Describing Variation in American Sign Language: Implicational Lects on the Deaf Diglossic Continuum

© 1994
James Woodward, Ph.D.

ROYALTIES

In November, 1993, the Research Committee of The Chinese University of Hong Kong, Shatin, New Territories, Hong Kong, under its Long-term Strategic Research Programme, approved a programme entitled Asian-Pacific Sign Languages/Deaf Studies Research and Training Programme. The CUHK Asian-Pacific Sign Languages/Deaf Studies Research and Training Program is a grant-supported, interdisciplinary research and training program that concentrates on Sign Language Linguistics, Sign Language Teaching, Sign Language Interpretation, Deaf Education, and Deaf Awareness. Research and training will first focus on Hong Kong and gradually expand in stages to include Southern China and Taiwan, Northern China, East Asia, Southeast Asia, South Asia, and the Pacific.

Since the Asian-Pacific Sign Languages/Deaf Studies Research and Training Programme will be funded primarily from extra mural sources, in December, 1993, The Chinese University of Hong Kong established a special donation account which will be used to support certain aspects of the Asian Pacific Sign Languages/Deaf Studies Research and Training Programme, especially projects related to the development of university level education programmes in Hong Kong for deaf students. This special donation account fund is called The CUHK Deaf Education Fund. All royalties from this book will go to The CUHK Deaf Education Fund.

TABLE OF CONTENTS

LIST OF TABLES vi
ACKNOWLEDGEMENTS ix
HISTORICAL PERSPECTIVE x

CHAPTER I
INTRODUCTION 1
1.1 General Remarks 1
1.2 Objectives 3
1.3 Some Notes on ASL Cherology 3

CHAPTER II
THE DEAF DIGLOSSIC CONTINUUM 13
2.1 The Deaf Community 13
2.2 Sign Language Diglossia 14
2.3 The Diglossic Continuum 15

CHAPTER III
VARIATION THEORY 17
3.1 Mainstream Linguistics 17
3.2 Dialectology 20
3.3 Sociolinguistics 20
3.4 The Development of Variation Theory 21
3.4.1 The Variable Rule 22
3.4.2 Implicational Analysis 24
3.4.3 Criticisms of the Two Models 25
3.4.4 The Wave Model 26
3.4.5 Panlectal and Polylectal Grammars 28
3.5 Summary 29
3.6 Conclusion 30

CHAPTER IV
FIELD METHODS 31
4.1 Data Gathering 31
4.1.1 Instruments 31
4.1.1.1 The Videotape 31
4.1.1.2 The Questionnaire 32
4.1.2 Informants 43
4.2 Procedure 45

CHAPTER V
VARIATION IN NEGATION 47
5.1 Negative Incorporation 47
5.1.1 Negative Incorporation Implication 47
5.1.2 Relation of Negative Incorporation Lects with Social Variables 52
5.1.3 Negative Incorporation Rule 55
5.2 Not Negation 57
5.2.1 Not Negation Implication 57
5.2.2 Relation of Not Negation Lects with Social Variables 61
5.2.3 Not Negation Rule 64

CHAPTER VI
VARIATION IN AGENT-BENEFICIARY DIRECTIONALITY 67
6.1 Outward-Inward Agent-Beneficiary Directionality 67
6.1.1 Outward-Inward Agent-Beneficiary Implication 67
6.1.2 Relation of Outward-Inward Agent-Beneficiary Lects with Social Variables 70
6.1.3 Outward-Inward Agent-Beneficiary Rule 77
6.2 Outward-Only Agent-Beneficiary Directionality 77
6.2.1 Outward-Only Agent-Beneficiary Implication 77
6.2.2 Relation of Outward-Only Agent-Beneficiary Lects with Social Variables 80
6.2.3 Outward-Only Agent-Beneficiary Rule 87

CHAPTER VII
VARIATION IN VERB REDUPLICATION 89
7.1 Verb Reduplication Implication 89
7.2 Relation of Verb Reduplication Lects with Social Variables 94
7.3 Verb Reduplication Rule 99

CHAPTER VIII
RESEARCH IMPLICATIONS 103
8.1 Results of the Study 103
8.1.1 The Implications 103
8.1.2 Relation of Implications with Social Variables 103
8.1.2.1 Negative Incorporation Lects 103

- 8.1.2.2 Not Negation Lects 104
- 8.1.2.3 Outward-Inward Agent-Beneficiary Lects 104
- 8.1.2.4 Outward-Only Agent-Beneficiary Lects............104
- 8.1.2.5 Verb Reduplication Lects 104
- 8.1.3 Cherological Features 105
- 8.2 Implications of the Study 105
- 8.2.1 Variation Theory 105
- 8.2.1.1 Implicational Analysis 105
- 8.2.1.2 Relation of Linguiistic Variation with Social Variation 106
- 8.2.2 American Sign Language.......................................106
- 8.3 Future Research 107
- 8.3.1 Other Locations and Informants 107
- 8.3.2 Other Variables 108
- 8.4 Final Remarks 108
- APPENDIX...111
- BIBLIOGRAPHY...121

LIST OF TABLES

1	Symbols Used for Writing ASL	4
2	A Tentative Representation of ASL Dezes	10
3	A Tentative Representation of ASL Tabs	11
4	Frequency of Application of the Hypothetical Variable Rule	23
5	Possible Lects with Four Features	25
6	Possible Lects with Four Features in Implicational Order	25
7	Implicational Patterns with Variation	27
8	Frequency Pattern	28
9	Classification of Informants by Social Variables	44
10	Implicational Lects for Negative Incorporation	50
11	Membership in Negative Incorporation Lects	51
12a	Membership in Negative Incorporation Lects Based on Deafness	52
12b	A 2 by 2 Representation of Table 12a	52
13a	Membership in Negative Incorporation Lects Based on Parentage	53
13b	A 2 by 2 Representation of Table 13a	53
14a	Membership in Negative Incorporation Lects Based on Age of Sign Language Acquisition	54
14b	A 2 by 2 Representation of Table 14a	54
15a	Membership in Negative Incorporation Lects Based on Education	54
15b	A 2 by 2 Representation of Table 15a	55
16a	Features on Negative Incorporation Verbs	56
16b	Weighted Features on Negative Incorp. Verbs	56
17	Implicational Lects for Not Negation	59
18	Membership in Not Negation Lects	60
19a	Membership in Not Negation Lects Based on Deafness	61
19b	A 2 by 2 Representation of Table 19a	62
20a	Membership in Not Negation Lects Based on Parentage	62
20b	A 2 by 2 Representation of Table 20a	62

21a	Membership in Not Negation Lects Based on Age of Sign Language Acquisition 63
21b	A 2 by 2 Representation of Table 21a 63
22a	Membership in Not Negation Lects Based on Education 64
22b	A 2 by 2 Representation on Table 22a 64
23	Weighted Features on Not Negation Verbs That May Take Negative Incorporation 65
24	Implicational Lects for Outward-Inward Agent-Beneficiary Directionality 69
25	Membership in Outward-Inward Agent-Beneficiary Lects 70
26a	Membership in Outward-Inward Agent-Beneficiary Lects by Deafness 71
26b	A 2 by 2 Representation of Table 26a 71
27a	Membership in Outward-Inward Agent-Beneficiary Lects by Parentage 72
27b	A 2 by 2 Representation of Table 27a 72
28a	Membership in Outward-Inward Agent-Beneficiary Lects by Age of Sign Language Acquisition 73
28b	A 2 by 2 Representation of Table 28a 73
29a	Membership in Outward-Inward Agent-Beneficiary Lects by Education 74
29b	A 2 by 2 Representation of Table 29a 74
30a	Features on Outward-Inward Agent-Beneficiary Verbs 75
30b	Weighted Features on Outward-Inward Agent-BeneficiaryVerbs 76
31	Implicational Lects For Outward-Only Agent-Beneficiary Lects 79
32	Membership in Outward-Only Agent-Beneficiary Lects 80
33a	Membership in Outward-Only Agent-Beneficiary Lects by Deafness 81
33b	A 2 by 2 Representation of Table 33a 81
34a	Membership in Outward-Only Agent-Beneficiary Lects by Parentage 82
34b	A 2 by 2 Representation of Table 34a 82

35a	Membership in Outward-Only Agent-Beneficiary Lects by Age of Sign Language Acquisition	83
35b	A 2 by 2 Representation of Table 35a	83
36a	Membership in Outward-Only Agent-Beneficiary Lects by Education	84
36b	A 2 by 2 Representation of Table 36a	84
37a	Features on Outward-Only Agent-BeneficiaryVerbs	85
37b	Weighted Features on Outward-Only Agent-Beneficiary Verbs	86
38	Implicational Lects For Verb Reduplication	92
39	Membership in Verb Reduplication Lects	93
40a	Membership in Verb Reduplication Lects Based on Deafness	94
40b	A 2 by 2 Representation of Table 40a	94
41a	Membership in Verb Reduplication Lects Based on Parentage	95
41b	A 2 by 2 Representation of Table 41a	95
42a	Membership in Verb Reduplication Lects Based on Age of Sign Language Acquisition	96
42b	A 2 by 2 Representation of Table 42a	96
43a	Membership in Verb Reduplication Lects Based on Education	97
43b	A 2 by 2 Representation of Table 43a	97
44a	Features on Reduplicated Verbs	98
44b	Weighted Features on Reduplicated Verbs	100
45	Exceptions to the Negative Incorporation Implication	111
46	Exceptions to the Not Negation Implication	111
47	Exceptions to the Outward-Inward Agent-Beneficiary Implication	112
48	Exceptions to the Outward-Only Agent-Beneficiary Implication	115
49	Exceptions to Verb Reduplication Implication	118

ACKNOWLEDGEMENTS

I would like to thank the following people for their aid in completing this study: Roger Shuy, Ralph Fasold, and William Stokoe for their continued encouragement and their helpful suggestions for improving content and expression; John Ennis, William Ennis, Steven Ackley, and Alan Barwiolik for help in locating informants; Barbara Kannapel for help in preparing the stimulus videotape; Bonnie Rosenblatt and Robert Zambrano for help in analyzing questionnaire responses; Sandra Barnhill for consultation on statistics; Jane Woodward for help in preparing the study for final typing; and Jean Lawler for typing the final manuscript in record time. Any imperfections in the study are in no way due to the people listed above—the imperfections lie instead in me and my stubbornness.

I would also like to thank the National Science Foundation for partial tuition support for my graduate studies and for support for research at Gallaudet College under research grant # GS-31349 and the National Institute of Mental Health for support for research at Gallaudet College under research grant # NS-10302-01.

HISTORICAL PERSPECTIVE

In 1992, Linstok Press began publishing its *Sign Language Dissertation Series,* which features unedited versions of key doctoral dissertations in Sign Language Linguistics. This dissertation, the first Linguistics Ph.D. dissertation on American Sign Language (see Cokely and Baker 1980, xvii), was approved by Roger W. Shuy, Ralph W. Fasold, and William C. Stokoe, Jr. on April 9, 1973, almost twenty years before the *Sign Language Dissertation Series* began and twenty-one years before the publication of this dissertation as part of the *Sign Language Dissertation Series.*

Depending on a number of factors, such as the observer's point of view and the object studied, twenty-one years can be seem like a relatively long time or a relatively short time. Since it is likely that many of the people reading this book will be university students and since many current undergraduate students, including the 302 undergraduates I have taught in Linguistics courses this academic year at The Chinese University of Hong Kong, were not even born at the time this dissertation was written, some historical perspective may be in order.

Perhaps this is especially true for many young deaf and hearing people in the United States, who do not remember the time when it was impossible in many places in the United States to study American Sign Language at the university level or to use American Sign Language to satisfy foreign or second language requirements at the undergraduate and/or postgraduate levels. It may be of interest to note that while The School of Languages and Linguistics at Georgetown University approved my request to write my Ph.D. dissertation on American Sign Language, they refused my request that I be allowed to use American Sign Language to satisfy my second language requirement for my Ph.D. Instead I used (Mandarin) Chinese, which for me at that time, was particularly ironic, since I had entered into the Linguistic study of American Sign Language precisely because I could not continue my original career goal of becoming a linguist who specialized in Chinese Linguistics.

There is a curious interconnection of Linguistics, Chinese, and sign languages that runs throughout much of my life and that as a consequence has affected much of my professional work, this dissertation included. Linguistics led me to Chinese; Chinese led me to American Sign Language (ASL); and ASL led me to this dissertation. Once this dissertation was completed, I realized that this study was only a small beginning toward describing variation in ASL and that much more work was needed. The dissertation led me to a number of other research studies; and the other research studies eventually led me back to Hong Kong and my current work on descriptive, sociolinguistic, and historical-comparative studies of sign languages in the Asian-Pacific region. From a Western philosophical perspective, I suppose it is possible to see this dissertation as a milestone towards a linear goal. But I prefer a more Taoist philosophical interpretation in which this dissertation serves as a focal and unifying reference point in my professional life which is not linear but cyclical in a multidimensional sense, where "before and after follow each other" (Lao Tzu, *Tao Te Ching,* Book 1,1:5) in tangent cycles or circles.

Before I go any further, I should point out that I did not actively search out a career related to the study of sign languages and deaf people. Rather circumstances in the path of my life brought me to a position where I could either choose to work with sign languages and deaf people or choose not to do so. Until I was twenty years of age, I lived in the United States and during that time, I never met a deaf person, and I had never (at least consciously) noticed any deaf people around me. In the Fall of 1968,1 moved to Hsinchu, Taiwan to live for one year. During this time, a deaf artist, selling his paintings, came to the house where I was living. I invited him in, "conversed" with him in written Chinese and bought some of his paintings Certainly not a momentous occasion, even in retrospect; but I believe it clearly shows that research on sign languages was not a topic on my agenda as late as 1968 although it clearly became one by 1969.

I came to Taiwan in the Fall of 1968 because I had finished all of my required courses in my major (Theoretical Linguistics) by the end of my third year of university in the Spring of 1968, and I had decided to try to improve my Mandarin Chinese by joining some classmates who were going to Taiwan. (I had earlier become interested in Mandarin as a result of my training in Linguistics. I wanted to be able to get some practical experience in a Non-lndo-European Language; and of the Non-lndo-European Languages offered at Georgetown University, Chinese interested me the most.) After spending my senior year abroad in Taiwan in 1968-69,1 decided to return to the United States and to get my Ph.D. in Chinese Linguistics at Georgetown University. With a scholarship (my first) in hand, I thought my future was pretty certain and predictable.

How wrong I was. The Vietnam War intervened in my life as it did in so many others of my generation, although (in my opinion) I was much more fortunate than most men my age. My draft lottery number was 18 as I remember, and by the time I had returned to the United States to graduate with my B.S. in June of 1969, my number had already come up for call. Graduate school deferments had ended, so I was forced to give up my scholarship. I had a choice of either volunteering for one of the armed services, waiting until I was called by the Selective Service System, or trying to find an occupational deferment. After my year of living in Taiwan, I did not agree with foreign policies that the United States was promoting in Asia and knew that I did not want to participate in a war I did not agree with. So, I tried to find a teaching position which might offer me a chance for some sort of alternative service and some possibility of continuing my graduate studies.

By the beginning of August, 1969 I had not found such a job and had received a letter ordering me to report for my army physical examination. A few days before the scheduled examination, I received a job offer from a defense contractor to prepare Vietnamese language teaching materials for the army. This was definitely not something I really wanted to do, especially since I had strong reasons to suspect that a good bit of the materials I would be preparing would be used for interrogation purposes. Quite frustrated, I went to the Chair of the Chinese Language Department at Georgetown University, explained my situation and asked for advice. The Chair asked me if I had tried calling Gallaudet College. I said that I had never heard of Gallaudet College and that they probably wouldn't hire me, because I had not completed my M.S. degree. The Chair said that Gallaudet College was a college for deaf students, that his wife had once taken a sign language course there from a teacher who had a B.A. degree, and that I should probably give it a try.

With two days left until my army physical, I called Gallaudet College. Having met only one deaf person in my life, the deaf artist in Taiwan, I knew that I knew little about deaf people, but I knew enough to figure out that Gallaudet College would probably have little need for a teacher specializing in Chinese Linguistics. So when the operator at the general switchboard number answered, I asked if there were any jobs teaching English or Linguistics. The operator connected me with William Stokoe, who was then Chair of the English Department. I asked if he had any jobs teaching English or Linguistics. He promptly responded that as a matter of fact he did, since someone had just come into his office and asked for a leave of absence. Bill said that he was leaving for a two-week vacation the next day, so if I was interested I could come over for an interview after his vacation. I explained that by the time he got back I would probably be in the army because I had my army physical in two days. Bill said that his vacation could wait a day and that I should come over the next day for an interview.

So, wanting to appear professional, I dressed up in one of my two suits (a three-piece one at that), took the bus to Gallaudet, and had a long, conversational "interview" with Bill Stokoe. Bill offered me the job on the spot because he needed someone immediately and also, I think, because I was the first person (to Bill's knowledge) with a degree in Linguistics to apply to work at Gallaudet College. As you might expect, I accepted the job offer immediately and immediately thereafter applied for an occupational deferment. While waiting to find out about my deferment, I had to go to the army physical, which, not to my surprise, I passed. I also had two weeks of special classes in "sign language" (Sign English, not American Sign Language). After my two weeks of "sign language" training, which included such helpful hints, such as "if you don't know a sign, just pantomime the concept," I was thrown into teach two first-year English courses and one graduate course in Introductory Linguistics without an interpreter, since all Gallaudet teachers were expected to sign for themselves (no matter how badly).

Realizing that in my native language variety that I "had pretty much done gone up shit creek without no paddle," I focused my energies on trying to find ways to learn ASL and to learn about ASL. I spent a great deal of time trying to interact with deaf people socially. I also spent some time thinking about how I could get the graduate training I now needed. I knew clearly that graduate studies in Chinese Linguistics was no longer a really viable option for me. Fortunately, I did not have to wait long before something more relevant came my way, the new Sociolinguistics Program at Georgetown University. I was able to transfer to this new program in the Fall of 1970, and it provided me with the theoretical framework on which this dissertation is based.

In 1971, the Linguistics Research Lab (LRL) became an autonomous unit at Gallaudet College (Cokely and Baker 1980, xvi). When Bill Stokoe took over full-time directorship of the LRL, he found grant money to release me from a large part of my teaching responsibilities in the English Department, and I was thus able to engage more actively in research work that was related to American Sign Language and Sociolinguistics. Occasionally I was able to discuss some of my research findings in public forums. When I would discuss such rules as Negative Incorporation and Agent-Beneficiary Directionality (one type of verb agreement) in American Sign Language, I would give examples of verbs which could take these rules. Invariably, there would be arguments among native signers about which verbs could take these rules and which could not. Then, some hearing person in the audience would stand up and say it was obvious that American Sign Language did not have a grammar, because even native signers couldn't agree on the rules. I would try to explain that it was my opinion that the rules were regular, but there was variation in the way different signers used the rules. I also explained that this was a common sociolinguistic phenomenon in many languages, including English, but that many people, including native users, tend to judge certain forms as more "standard" than others and that certain "non-standard" forms were said to be "incorrect" and ignored in most studies of most languages.

Needless to say, this made little impact on most people, especially since at that time I had very little empirical data to support my arguments. So, I decided that if I was going to make my case for the regularity not only of ASL rules but also the regularity of variation in ASL rules, I might as well do my dissertation on this topic. I believed (and still do believe) that Variation Theory in Sociolinguistics and the structure and use of ASL, as well as the structure and use of most vernacular minority group language varieties (both signed and spoken), were made for each other. In fact I think that the concurrent development of Variation Theory and of the Linguistic study of sign languages was hardly coincidental, given the environment of the late 60's and early 70's. Similarly, it's not much of a coincidence to note that this dissertation is simultaneously the first Ph.D. Linguistics dissertation on American Sign Language and the first Ph.D. dissertation from the Sociolinguistics Program at Georgetown University. Soon after this dissertation was completed, a number of other graduate students focused on Sociolinguistics and American Sign Language, also in the Sociolinguistics Program at Georgetown University. Interestingly, all of the subsequent hearing graduate students interested in Sociolinguistics were able to use American Sign Language to satisfy their second language requirements for the Ph.D. In a parallel fashion, deaf graduate students in Sociolinguistics at Georgetown University were able to use English to satisfy their second language requirements.

As for me, my completed dissertation was both an end and a beginning or perhaps several ends and beginnings, all happening simultaneously. The dissertation brought my graduate study to a close and opened up the possibility of a long-term academic career in university teaching and research. It brought to an end (or so I thought at the time) the possibility of working in Asia and focused my attention on the implications for future research suggested by the findings of the dissertation. Because of the highly specialized nature of the dissertation, I did not bother to even try to look for a publisher, but instead, published three summary articles, one on Verb Reduplication (Woodward 1973a), one on Negative Incorporation (Woodward 1974a), and one on Agent-Beneficiary Directionality (Woodward 1975). I also decided that it would be interesting to compare the responses of individuals across implications in the study and produced a study of the results of the interrule implicational study (Woodward 1973b). Following the research implications outlined in the dissertation, I also did a replication of the study in other areas in the United States (Woodward 1974b), and decided to look more closely at phonological implications in various regional and ethnic groups in the United States (Battison, Markowicz, and Woodward 1975; Woodward and Erting 1975; Woodward, Erting and Oliver 1976; Woodward 1976; Woodward and De Santis 1977a) and in

France (Woodward 1979a; Woodward and De Santis 1977b). An article including a detailed summary of sociolinguistic studies of implicational variation in ASL and the implications of these studies for bilingual education for deaf students was published somewhat later (Woodward 1980).

Also related to education was the large scale study of classroom communication practices that was developed through collaborative work with the Center for Assessment and Demographic Studies at Gallaudet University. The questionnaire for this research was developed as suggested in this dissertation using implications to measure and assess language competence. Articles resulting from this research includes articles which focus specifically on implicational analysis (Woodward and Allen 1986, 1993a, 1993b; Woodward 1990) and articles which make inferences from implicational analysis (Woodward, Allen, and Schildroth 1985; Woodward and Allen 1987, 1988).

In a somewhat different vein, although still following some of the implications for research that were outlined in the dissertation, I also started to work on implicational universals in sign language phonology (Woodward 1978a, 1979b, 1981, 1982, 1985, 1987) and semantics (Woodward 1978b, 1989).

This focus on phonological and semantic universals, along with earlier historical work on American and French sign languages, led me back to an interest in the historical-comparative relationships of sign languages. While I thought I would be able to focus my efforts in historical-comparative research on sign languages in Latin America, this ultimately proved to be impossible. In searching for other opportunities to do historical-comparative research, I found an employment opportunity at The Chinese University of Hong Kong.

And so again, it appears like another end and another beginning but certainly not a substantially different end nor a substantially different beginning. Again I find myself teaching Linguistics in an English Department and working on Sign Language Linguistics in another Linguistics Research Lab. In addition, I am again in a place where little Sign Language Linguistics has been done, where much needs to be done, and where there is a need to develop a comprehensive program in Sign Language Linguistics. It all feels very familiar somehow, and the publication of this dissertation at this stage in my life makes it feel even more so. The difference is I feel I am finally coming back home. My Mandarin is very rusty, but a surprising amount is still there. My Cantonese is barely at survival level, and I have to start from the beginning in learning Hong Kong Sign Language. But in spite of these difficulties, it feels very right and very comfortable to be living in Asia again.

At this point, the present, this written historical perspective must end, although I am still actively working on research suggested by this dissertation, a dictionary of Black Southern Varieties of American Sign Language that is being completed as a result of a grant from the U.S. National Endowment for the Humanities.

I hope this historical perspective has provided the necessary context for reading this document, which was prepared twenty-one years ago, a time in which most linguists still agreed with the traditional view of Bloomfield, one of the founders of autonomous modern American linguistics, that "gesture languages (that) have been observed among deaf-mutes (sic) are merely developments of ordinary gestures and that any and all complicated or not immediately intelligible gestures are based on the conventions of ordinary speech (Bloomfield 1965, 39)....elaborate systems of gesture, deaf and dumb language (sic), signaling codes, the use of writing, telegraphy, and so on, turn out, upon inspection to be merely derivative of (spoken) language (Bloomfield 1965, 144)"; a time when it was possible to write a Ph.D. dissertation about a sign language, but not necessarily possible to use the same language to satisfy second language requirements for the Ph.D.; a time when a bibliography of sign language references included almost as many manuscripts as published articles; in short, a time when we all knew much less than we know today.

Yet, while we have learned much more about certain aspects of certain varieties of American Sign Language, many sign language researchers and sign language teachers still tend to gloss over variation or fail to treat variation as a serious and important topic. As a result, we still have some of the following situations: 1) supposedly proficient signers and/or interpreters who cannot understand "nonstandard" forms of ASL, especially those forms used by older Black and White Southern signers; 2) hearing, non-native interpreters who try to "correct" the signs of native or near-native Black Southern signers, 3) White, college educated, middle class native ASL users who propose that any deaf person who signs differently from them doesn't know ASL, among others. On a more humorous note, I have had some deaf and hearing native ASL users claim that I must have made up the sign data used in this dissertation, because they had never seen any deaf person use some of the signs I found native deaf signers using. But, of course, I certainly didn't have to make up any signs. The variations that these people claimed don't exist were exactly what prompted me to do the study in the first place. I feel it is likely I will get similar responses from some people who will read the forthcoming dictionary of Black Southern Varieties of ASL, which is tentatively entitled, *Beauty From Hate: The Development and Death of Black Southern Varieties of American Sign Language*. I am sure that the great majority of both deaf and hearing White native users of ASL have never seen the great majority of signs that will be included in the dictionary. Just because a native user of a language has never seen a form does not mean it does not exist. That's the whole point of the forthcoming book, of this book, and of indeed of any studies in Variation Theory which use polylectal and/or panlectal grammars. A panlectal grammar, by its very nature, posits that a grammar of a language is beyond the control of any individual native user of the language productively and even receptively. No one individual, no matter how proficient he or she may be can hope to be a model or a judge for grammaticality of the language as a whole. Variation, even variation we as individual native users have never seen, still exists and will continue to exist, regardless of how we may feel about it. We can choose to deal with the variation or not to deal with it.

If we choose to deal with variation, it is possible to use information found in this dissertation as one possibility for describing and explaining variation in American Sign Language. Later developments in Sociolinguistics provide other related possibilities.

If we choose not to deal with variation, we can simply ignore the variation that is around us, deny that it exists, or even denigrate it as "non-standard" or "ungrammatical"; but again it is important to point out that none of this makes variation go away, it just conveniently puts it where we don't have to deal with it. But every action and even every inaction has consequences. If we choose not to deal with variation, someone will suffer the consequences. The someone could be an interpreter who cannot understand a deaf client whose signs vary significantly from what the interpreter knows or has been taught. The someone could be an interpreter who even thinks s/he can understand the client and actually can't. The someone could be the deaf client who isn't understood and suffers because of it. The someone could simply be ourselves who miss understanding the beautiful but integrate tapestry of regional, social, ethnic, age, and gender variation that makes competence in ASL or any other language beyond the power of any one individual user.

James Woodward
Linguistics Research Laboratory
The Chinese University of Hong Kong

Shatin, New Territories, Hong Kong
March, 1994

References Cited

Battison, R., H. Markowicz, and J. Woodward
    1975 A Good Rule of Thumb: Variable Phonology in American Sign Language. In R. Fasold & R. Shuy (eds.) *Analyzing Variation in Language.* Washington, D.C.: Georgetown University Press, 191-302.

Bloomfield, L.
    1965 *Language.* New York: Holt, Rinehart and Winston. (Original copyright 1933, copyright renewed 1961, 1965 published version.)

Cokely, D. and C. Baker
    1980 Sign Language in the 20th Century: A Chronology. In C. Baker and R. Battison (eds.) *Sign Language and the Deaf Community.* Silver Spring, MD: National Association of the Deaf, xv-xx.

Woodward, J.
    1973a Some Observations on Sociolinguistic Variation and American Sign Language. *Kansas Journal of Sociology* 9:2, 191-200.
    1973b Interrule Implication in American Sign Language. *Sign Language Studies* 3, 47- 56.
    1974a Implicational Variation in American Sign Language:

Negative Incorporation. *Sign Language Studies* 5, 20-30.

1974b A Report on Montana-Washington Implicational Research. *Sign Language Studies* 4, 77-101.

1975 Variation in American Sign Language Syntax: Agent-Beneficiary Directionality. In R. Fasold & R. Shuy (eds.) *Analyzing Variation in Language.* Washington, D.C.: Georgetown University Press, 303-311.

1976 Black Southern Signing. *Language in Society* 5:1, 211-218.

1978a Signs of Marking: "Stage" Four Handshapes. A paper presented at the Summer Meeting of the Linguistic Society of America, Urbana.

1978b All in the Family: Kinship Lexicalization Across Sign Languages. *Sign Language Studies 19,* 121 - 138.

1979a Quelques Aspects Sociolinguistiques des Langues des Signes Americaine et Francaise. In F. Grosjean and H. Lane (eds.) *La Langue des Signes,Langages,* 56, 78-91.

1979b Crossing: Towards a Theory of Naturalness in Sign Language Phonology. A paper presented at the Winter Meeting of the Linguistic Society of America, Los Angeles.

1980 Some Sociolinguistic Problems in the Implementation of Bilingual Education for Deaf Students. In F. Caccamise and D. Hicks (eds.) *Proceedings of the Second National Symposium on Sign Language and Research and Teaching.* Silver Spring, MD: National Association of the Deaf, 183-203.

1981 Signs of Marking: "Stage" Three Handshapes. In M. Danesi (ed.) *Issues in Language: Studies in Honor of Robert J. DiPietro Presented to him by his Students.* Edward Sapir Monograph Series in Language, Culture, and Cognition, 9. Lake Bluff, IL: Jupiter Press, 47-59.

1982 Single Finger Extension: Towards a Theory of Naturalness in Sign Language Phonology. *Sign Language Studies* 37, 289-304.

1985 Universal Constraints on Two Finger Extension in Sign Languages. *Sign Language Studies* 46, 53-72.

1987 Universal Constraints Across Sign Languages: Single Finger Contact Handshapes. *Sign Language Studies*

57, 375-385.

1989 Basic Color Term Lexicalization Across Sign Languages. *Sign Language Studies* 63, 145-152.

1990 Sign English in the Education of Deaf Students. In H. Bornstein (ed.) *Manual Commununication: Implications for Education.* Washington, D.C.: Gallaudet University Press, 67-80

Woodward, J. and T. Allen

1986 Two Analyses of the ASL to English Continuum. In S. Delancey and R. Tomlin (eds.) *Proceedings of the Second Annual Meeting of the Pacific Linguistics Conference.* Eugene, Oregon: University of Oregon, Department of Linguistics, 471-497.

1987 Classroom Use of ASL by Teachers. *Sign Language Studies 54,* 1-10.

1988 Classroom Use of Artificial Sign Systems by Teachers. *Sign Language Studies* 61, 405-418

1993a Models of Deafness Compared: A Sociolinguistic Study of Deaf and Hard of Hearing Teachers. *Sign Language Studies 79,* 113-126.

1993b Sociolinguistic Differences: U.S. Teachers in Residential Schools and Non-Residential Schools. *Sign Language Studies* 81, 361 - 374.

Woodward, J., T. Allen, and A. Schildroth

1985 Teachers and Deaf Students: An Ethnography of Classroom Communication. In S. Delancey and R. Tomlin (eds.) Proceedings of the First Annual Meeting of the Pacific Linguistics Conference. Eugene, Oregon: University of Oregon, Department of Linguistics, 479-483.

Woodward, J. and S. De Santis

1977a Two To One It Happens: Dynamic Phonology in Two Sign Languages. *Sign Language Studies* 17, 319-346.

1977b Negative Incorporation in French and American Sign Languages. *Language in Society* 6:3, 379-388.

Woodward, .J. and C. Erting

1975 Synchronic Variation and Historical Change in American Sign Language. *Language Sciences,* 37, 9-12.

Woodward, J., C. Erting, and S. Oliver

1976 Facing and Handling Variation in American Sign Language Phonology. *Sign Language Studies* 10, 43-51.

Chapter I
Introduction

1.1 General Remarks.

Two basic areas of scholarly concern are developing concurrently: variability in Linguistics and interest in variation in American Sign Language.

The recent developments in variation theory propose to offer insights into explaining variation and historical change in language. Variation theory, in fact, challenges old assumptions about the validity of static synchronic descriptions of language. However, because variation theory is so new, relatively little research has been done in the dynamic framework of the variationists. This study on a visual language phenomenon, quite different from what linguists usually observe, should provide a crucial testing ground for the descriptive and explanatory power of the theory.

This study not only provides a testing ground for variation theory but also demonstrates further proof that American Sign Language is indeed a language and as such has a systematic grammar and cherology.

For a long time, because of ethnocentric attitudes, hearing critics have denied that American Sign Language exists or have stated that it is parasitic on English grammar and is only poor English grammar. As Markowicz (1972), Stokoe (1970, 1972a), and others have pointed out, this ethnocentrism has pervaded much of deaf education, certainly not to the benefit of the deaf. Unfortunately, many linguists in their ignorance about sign languages have not challenged these ethnocentric ideas and indeed many linguists have succumbed themselves to the same ideas because of their preoccupation with oral language. Markowicz (1972: 35-36) states the problem well:

> The similarity between the criticisms of sign language and of nonstandard Negro English is striking. Labov points out that "linguists have endeavored for many years to show that differences in language are matters of social convention established by historical processes which shift continually the social prestige of dialect variants" (Labov, 1970a: 1). Apparently, they have not been too successful in disseminating this point of view since the opposite opinion prevails in our society. The argument for equal status for sign language is more difficult to present since, in one extreme, it is an independent language, and in the other, it is a visual representation of English, both varieties making use of signs. The prejudice against nonstandard English dialects is caused by "ignorance of basic facts about human language and the people who speak it" (Labov, 1970a: 34). To make sign language acceptable requires, in addition, overcoming the long standing assumption concerning the relation of thinking and spoken language. In this respect, structural linguists (Stokoe excepted) have been of no help, because to do so would cause them to contradict their underlying assumption, namely, that thinking is a silent expression of speech.

This study demonstrates that although American Sign Language has been influenced by spoken English (as indeed Signed and Manual English have been influenced by American Sign Language), American Sign Language has systemically observable and describable differences from English, and these are conditioned by semantic and/or cherological, i.e., mutatis mutandis, phonological, constraints.

It is the conditioning of American Sign Language grammatical variation by cherological constrains that, I believe, offers the strongest statement for the autonomy of American Sign Language. The cherology of American Sign Language cannot be shown to come from or have a one-to-one relationship with English phonology. Thus variation in the unique and autonomous set of grammar rules of American Sign Language is being conditioned by unique and autonomous sets of cherological features.

1.2 Objectives.

This study then has two major objectives: (1) to determine if variation in American Sign Language is regular and rule-governed and (2) to determine if variation theory is adequate to describe and explain this variation.

The remaining chapters offer both the theoretical framework for discussion of these objectives and data to demonstrate that variation in American Sign Language is regular and rule-governed and that variation theory is not only adequate to explain this variation but also offers insights which traditional static approaches do not offer.

However, before any data in American Sign Language can be presented, it will be necessary to review recent research in American Sign Language cherology. There are two reasons for this: (1) a knowledge of the cherological transcription system is a necessary prerequisite for reading the data and (2) cherological feature analysis is used in writing generative polylectal rules later in the paper.

1.3 Some Notes on ASL Cherology.

Stokoe (1960, 1965) did a cheremic analysis of American Sign Language. He showed that sign cheremes could be classified into three major groups: tabs or the places where signs are made, dezes or the hand shapes used in making signs, and sigs or the motions involved in making signs. His transcription system, presented in Table 1, is used in transcribing signs in this paper.

Table 1
SYMBOLS USED FOR WRITING THE SIGNS OF THE AMERICAN SIGN LANGUAGE

Tab symbols

1. ∅   zero, the neutral place where the hands move, in contrast with all places below
2. ∩̬   face or whole head
3. ∩   forehead or brow, upper face
4. ⊔   mid-face, the eye and nose region
5. ∪   chin, lower face
6. }   cheek, temple, ear, side-face
7. π   neck
8. [ ]   trunk, body from shoulders to hips
9. \   upper arm
10. ∕   elbow, forearm
11. α   wrist, arm in supinated position (on its back)
12. ᴅ   wrist, arm in pronated position (face down)

Dez symbols, some also used as tab

13. A   compact hand, fist; may be like 'a', 's', or 't' of manual alphabet
14. B   flat hand
15. 5   spread hand; fingers and thumb spread like '5' of manual numeration
16. C   curved hand; may be like 'c' or more open
17. E   contracted hand; like 'e' or more clawlike

Table 1 (continued)

18.	F	"three-ring" hand; from spread hand, thumb and index finger touch or cross
19.	G	index hand; like 'g' or sometimes like 'd'; index finger points from fist
20.	H	index and second finger, side by side, extended
21.	I	"pinkie" hand; little finger extended from compact hand
22.	K	like G except that thumb touches middle phalanx of second finger; like 'k' and 'p' of manual alphabet
23.	L	angle hand; thumb, index finger in right angle, other fingers usually bent into palm
24.	3	"cock" hand; thumb and first two fingers spread, like '3' of manual numeration
25.	O	tapered hand; fingers curved and squeezed together over thumb; may be like 'o' of manual alphabet
26.	R	"warding off" hand; second finger crossed over index finger, like 'r' of manual alphabet
27.	V	"victory" hand; index and second fingers extended and spread apart
28.	W	three-finger hand; thumb and little finger touch, others extended spread
29.	X	hook hand; index finger bent in hook from fist, thumb tip may touch fingertip

Table 1 (continued)

30.	Y	"horns" hand; thumb and little finger spread out extended from fist; or index and little fingers extended, parallel
31.	8	(allocheric variant of Y); second finger bent in from spread hand, thumb may touch fingertip

Sig symbols

32.	∧	upward movement
33.	∨	downward movement
34.	N	up-and-down movement
35.	>	rightward movement
36.	<	leftward movement
37.	z	side to side movement
38.	T	movement toward signer
39.	⊥	movement away from signer
40.	I	to-and-fro movement
41.	a	supinating rotation (palm up)
42.	ʋ	pronating rotation (palm down)
43.	ω	twisting movement
44.	η	nodding or bending action
45.	◻	opening action (final dez configuration shown in brackets)
46.	♯	closing action (final dez configuration shown in brackets)
47.	ᚱ	wiggling action of fingers

Table 1 (continued)

48.	ඉ	circular action
49.	)(	convergent action, approach
50.	X	contactual action, touch
51.	⊐C	linking action, grasp
52.	✦	crossing action
53.	⊙	entering action
54.	÷	divergent action, separate
55.	⟨⟩	interchanging action

(Stokoe et al. 1965: X-XII)

Bellugi (1972), using George Miller's methodology for short term memory tests demonstrated that these sign phonemes are as psychologically and linguistically real as sound phonemes.

Battison, Friedman, and Zambrano (1972) have attempted a feature analysis of dezes. These researchers discovered that the following features were necessary to describe dezes:

+closed   some of the fingers are closed into a fist
−closed   none of the fingers are closed into a fist

+thumb   the thumb is extended
−thumb   the thumb is not extended

+spread   extended fingers are spread
−spread   extended fingers are not spread

+bent   extended fingers are bent
−bent   extended fingers are not bent

+fore   the forefinger is extended
−fore   the forefinger is not extended

+mid   the mid finger is extended
−mid   the mid finger is not extended

+ring   the ring finger is extended
−ring   the ring finger is not extended

+pinky   the little finger is extended
−pinky   the little finger is not extended

+contact   one or more fingers touch the thumb
−contact   one or more fingers do not touch the thumb

+crossed   fingers are crossed
−crossed   fingers are not crossed

    While these features are still considered highly speculative by the researchers, they proved to be extremely useful in the construction of rules with weighted features in the analysis of the linguistic variables in this study. Table 2 on page 10 shows the actual feature analysis of dezes.

    Battison and Woodward (1972) attempted a feature analysis of tabs. While these features are also considered highly speculative, they also proved to be extremely useful in rule writing in this study. The researchers found that the following features were necessary to describe tabs:

+body   the body is touched
−body   the body is not touched

+appendage   directly connected to the trunk (head and arms)
−appendage   not directly connected to the trunk (Ø tab, trunk, hands)

+flexible   can be flexed (arms and hands)
−flexible   cannot be flexed (Ø tab, trunk and head)

+facial feature	between the eyebrows and lips (inclusive)
−facial feature	not between the eyebrows and lips
+high	high in relation to a specific part of the body (defined by ± appendage, ± body, ± flexible)
−high	not high
+low	low in relation to a specific part of the body
−low	not low
+extreme	at boundaries of a specific part of the body
−extreme	not at boundaries of a specific part of body
+ipse	the same side of the body as the hand(s) making the sign
−ipse	not the same side of the body as the hand(s) making the sign
+contra	the opposite side of the body from the hand(s) making the sign
−contra	not the opposite side of the body from the hand(s) making the sign

Table 3 shows the feature analysis of tabs.

To date no feature analysis of sigs has been attempted, but further research in American Sign Language cherology is presently being carried out by Battison and Friedman, under a National Endowment for the Humanities Youth Grant. Since the project has just begun, there is no information on their progress.

TABLE 2
A TENTATIVE FEATURE REPRESENTATION OF ASL DEZES

	S	E	O	C	B	4	T	A	A	B	B₁	5	5	⋮	G	X	D	Gₐ	G	L	I	Y	7	8	H	N	V	R	3	K	M	W	6	F	9	Fₛ	Mₜ	Nₜ
Closed	+	+	-	-	-	-	+	+	+	-	-	-	-		-	-	-	+	+	+	+	+	-	-	+	+	+	+	+	+	+	-	-	-	-	+	+	+
Thumb	-	-	-	-	-	-	-	+	+	+	+	+	+		+	-	-	+	-	+	-	+	-	-	-	-	-	+	+	-	-	-	-	-	-	-	-	-
Spread	-	-	-	+	-	+	-	+	-	-	-	+	-		-	-	-	-	+	+	-	-	+	-	+	-	+	-	+	+	-	+	-	-	-	+	-	-
Bent	-	-	+	-	-	-	+	-	+	-	-	-	-		-	+	+	+	-	-	-	-	+	+	-	+	-	-	-	+	+	-	-	-	-	-	+	+
Fore	-	-	+	+	+	+	+	-	-	+	+	+	+		-	+	+	+	+	-	-	-	+	+	+	+	+	+	+	+	+	+	+	+	+	+	+	+
Mid	-	+	+	+	+	+	-	-	-	+	+	+	+		-	-	+	-	-	-	-	-	-	-	+	+	+	+	+	+	+	+	+	+	+	+	+	+
Ring	-	+	+	+	+	+	-	-	-	+	+	+	+		-	-	-	-	-	-	-	-	+	-	+	-	-	-	-	+	+	-	+	+	+	+	+	-
Pinky	-	+	+	+	+	+	-	-	-	+	+	+	+		-	-	-	-	-	-	-	+	+	+	+	+	-	-	-	-	-	-	+	+	+	-	-	-
Contact	-	+	-	-	-	-	-	-	-	-	-	-	-		-	-	-	+	-	-	-	-	+	+	-	-	-	-	+	-	-	-	+	+	+	+	-	-
Crossed	-	-	-	-	-	-	+	-	-	-	-	-	-		-	-	-	-	-	-	-	-	-	-	-	-	+	+	-	-	-	-	-	-	-	-	+	-

TABLE 3
A TENTATIVE REPRESENTATION OF ASL TABS

1. Top of Head
2. Forehead
3. Ipse Eye
4. Contra Eye
5. Ipse Nose
6. Center Nose
7. Contra Nose
8. Ipse Lips
9. Center Lips
10. Chin
11. Cheek (Ipse)
12. Ear (Ipse)
13. Neck
14. Ipse Shoulder
15. Contra Shoulder
16. Ipse High Trunk
17. Contra High Trunk
18. Center Chest
19. Ipse Low Trunk
20. Contra Low Trunk
21. High Arm (Contra)
22. Elbow (Contra)
23. Lower Arm (Contra)
24. Wrist (Contra)
25. Hand (See dezes)
26. Upper Leg (Ipse)
27. Zero Tab

TABLE 3
A TENTATIVE REPRESENTATION OF ASL TABS

	1	2	3	4	5	6	7	8	9	10	11	12	13	14	15	16	17	18	19	20	21	22	23	24	25	26	27
body	+	+	+	+	+	+	+	+	+	+	+	+	+	+	+	+	+	+	+	+	+	+	+	+	+	+	−
flexible	−	−	−	−	−	−	−	−	−	−	−	−	−	−	−	−	−	−	−	−	+	+	+	+	+	−	−
appendage	+	+	+	+	+	+	+	+	+	+	+	+	+	−	−	−	−	−	−	−	+	+	+	+	−	−	−
facial feature	−	−	+	+	+	+	+	+	+	−	−	−	−	−	−	−	−	−	−	−	−	−	−	−	−	−	−
high	+	−	−	−	−	−	−	−	−	−	−	−	−	+	+	+	+	−	−	−	+	+	−	−	−	−	−
low	−	−	−	−	−	−	−	+	+	+	−	−	+	−	−	−	−	−	+	+	−	−	+	+	−	+	−
extreme	+	−	−	−	−	−	−	−	−	+	−	+	+	+	+	−	−	−	−	−	+	−	−	+	−	+	−
ipse	−	−	+	−	+	−	−	+	−	−	+	+	−	+	−	+	−	−	+	−	−	−	−	−	−	+	−
contra	−	−	−	+	−	−	+	−	−	−	−	−	−	−	+	−	+	−	−	+	+	+	+	+	+	−	−

Chapter II
The Deaf Diglossic Continuum

2.1 The Deaf Community.

Croneberg (1965) and Meadow (1972) have pointed out that the deaf form a minority community in the United States. The deaf as a group are held together by language, clubs, social organizations, etc. (Meadow, 1972). She states:

> the group definition is strengthened further with the knowledge that deaf persons are characterized by endogamous marital patterns. In the survey of the deaf population of New York State, for example, it was found that only 5 per cent of women born deaf, and about 9 per cent of women who became deaf at an early age, were married to hearing men (Rainer, et al., 1963: 17). Voluntary associations include a National Association of the Deaf with many thousands of members and a semi-monthly publication, *The Deaf American*. In addition most states have subsidiary associations with publications of their own. State residential schools for the deaf form a nationwide network that supports the cohesiveness of the sub-culture and promotes language. Also in existence is a national deaf sports organization that sends delegates to the World Deaf Olympics, a deaf fraternal order with the primary purpose of offering special insurance for members, and innumerable local deaf social clubs and sports teams (Meadow, 1972: 2-3).

But just as not all Blacks belong to the U. S. Black subculture, not all the deaf belong to the deaf subculture. They must be enculturated or acculturated into the deaf community. Meadow points out that this socialization into the language and culture of the deaf community may take place at several times during the life of a deaf person. Meadow (1972: 14) writes, "These are (1) infancy; (2) the time of enrollment in a residential school for the deaf (probably between the ages of five and thirteen); (3) the time of graduation from high school." She later points out that deaf children of deaf parents generally are socialized into the deaf community at infancy and that deaf children of hearing parents are generally socialized at stage 2 or 3. But socialization into the deaf community *invariably* includes acquisition of some variety or varieties of language used by deaf community.

2.2 Sign Language Diglossia.

The language situation that acts as a cohesive force in the deaf community is a diglossic situation. Stokoe (1970) first pointed out the existence of diglossia in the deaf community, using Ferguson's (1959) classic paper on diglossia as a model. Stokoe defined the H variety as Manual English and the L variety as American Sign Language. Manual English is a combination of signs and fingerspelling that represents a morpheme to morpheme correlation with spoken English. An example of this is:

[] I ^{x} WENT $G_{T_{\text{p}}}$ $\underline{G}_{D}{}^{\text{x}}$ THE $Q_{\vee} Q_{\vee} \underline{\eta}$ ··

"I went to the store" where "I" is signed, "went" is fingerspelled, "to" is signed, "the" is fingerspelled, and "store" is signed.

All of these morphemes could be spelled and this would be what is known as the Rochester Method. American Sign Language is a language in and of itself. It has a different grammatical structure from English and has little, if any, fingerspelling. For example, English "Have you been to California?" which is Auxiliary, Subject, Verb, Locational Prepositional Phrase is translated into American Sign Language as:

$\mathcal{D}\ 8^{\text{x}}$ $BB^{\dot{\mathcal{D}}}$ $\}F^{\text{I}}\text{::}\emptyset\ Y^{\omega}$ $G^{\perp}$

"Touch finish California you?" which is Verb, Auxiliary, Locational Noun, Subject, and Question, where Subject and Question are signed simultaneously.

Stokoe, in the same article, also demonstrated that Manual English (H) and American Sign Language (L) have the sociolinguistic characteristics that languages in diglossic situations have. H is used in formal conversation, such as in church, the classroom, lectures, etc. L is used in smaller, less formal, more intimate conversations. H is considered superior to L, and L is regarded as ungrammatical or non-existent. Signers generally feel that "grammatical" H should be used instead of L for teaching. Some feel that standardization is necessary, but sign language diglossia appears as stable as other diglossic situations.

The diglossic situation that Stokoe is describing is not the "classical" diglossic situation, since as Ferguson (1959, 1972) has pointed out, the language varieties in diglossia that he was describing were actually varieties of the same language. However, Ferguson (1972) has also stated that although he does not particularly agree with the use of diglossia for situations where varieties of two different languages are involved Fishman and others, e.g. Stokoe, are using diglossia to refer to these situations.

2.3 The Diglossic Continuum.

Stokoe's (1970) treatment of diglossia in the deaf community concentrated primarily on the extreme ends of the diglossic situation. In actuality, there is a continuum existing between varieties of Manual English and American Sign Language (Stokoe, 1972, Woodward, 1972, and Moores, 1972). Intermediate varieties on the continuum have received various names: Deaf Non-standard English (Woodward, 1972), Signed English (O'Rourke, 1970) and Siglish (Fant, 1972).

Examples of Deaf Non-standard English are found in the written English of the deaf. These well known linguistic variables are commonly known as "errors" or "poor English" in deaf education, just as Black English as been called "poor English" by some educators. Some of these variables are deletion and/or hypercorrection of articles, "he is humorous sport" or "I have a bread"; deletion of third person singular /s "he go to store" and others. Because of the negative reactions of earlier educators to what seems to be Deaf Non-standard English, we know little about social variables that may condition this linguistic variation.

Undoubtedly some social variables are: social class, educational level of parents and self, date and degree of hearing loss of parents and self, whether the type of school attended was manual or oral, and probably a number of other factors.

Pidgin Sign English is another term for O'Rourke's (1971) Signed English and Fant's (1971) Siglish. Sometimes people sign something that seems to be a pidginized version of English. The syntactic order is primarily English, but inflections have been reduced in redundancy, and there is a mixture of American Sign Language and English structure. This pidgin seems always to be a second language, as expected of a pidgin, and is used only in restricted situations. An example of this pidgin is:

[] I ˣ   B̄₊   B ᐳ ˇ   ᴜG_∧ ⊥   G₊G< ⁰̃   G_T ₀   G_D ˣ   Q Q ˀ ··

"I finish be(en) go to store". "Finish" is an American Sign Language aspect marker, "be(en)" is an English word that is either spelled or signed, (Note there is not copula or progressive "be" in American Sign Language, so this is a purely English construction.), and "go" has the "ing" deleted.

Moores (1972) has also suggested the possibility that some varieties of Home Signs may well also be on the deaf diglossic continuum. He states: "At the lowest level a system might consist of home-made gestures invented and understood perhaps by only one class of six or even seven students in a classroom excluding parents, teachers, and even other deaf students in the same program" (Moores, 1972: 3). No studies have been done on Home Signs to date, so it is not known whether Home Signs constitute a developing linguistic system with duality of patterning and semantactic rules of its own, or whether it is merely a system of naming. With all the prejudices against studying a more or less standard variety of American Sign Language, one can easily see why Home Signs have been ignored, although one can hardly excuse such an attitude.

In summary, then, the deaf language situation has been described as a diglossic continuum. Unfortunately, however, no real effort has been made to do any linguistic description of this continuum utilizing recent developments in variation theory. This study attempts to utilize variation theory in analyzing the complex but regular variation that exists on the deaf diglossic continuum.

Chapter III
Variation Theory

3.1 Mainstream Linguistics.

From the founding of modern linguistics, one statement has been considered axiomatic about language: Language changes. De Saussure (1959) proposed the division of synchronic from diachronic linguistics. A synchronic linguistic study is a study of language at a frozen stage in its history. Diachronic studies are concerned with the comparison of two or more synchronic stages of a language.

The reason for this synchronic-diachronic dichotomy can be found in De Saussure's distinction of *la langue* and *la parole*. *Langue* is a social fact; it is the grammatical constraints on all users of a language. *Parole* is the individual's speech acts which are not social facts, but supposedly individual variations in performance. De Saussure

> goes on to add that his definition of *langue* "supposes our setting aside all that is foreign to its organism, its system, in a word, everything that is referred to by the term 'external linguistics'" (1962: 40; 1959: 20). He allows that external linguistics incudes many important things, especially linguistic matters that have to do with ethnology. He also mentions matters that today might be referred to as the *sociology of language*. And then he lists everything that has to do with "the geographical extension of the tongues and dialectal splitting" (1962: 41; 1959: 21), in short, what has traditionally been called *dialectology*. While conceding the merits of the study of "external linguistic phenomena" (1962: 42; 1959: 22), Saussure firmly denies the validity of the view that the internal linguistic organ-

ism cannot be known without studying such external phenomena (Bailey, 1971: 2).

Later linguists have generally accepted the *langue-parole* distinction as Bailey (1971) points out in the same work. For example, the structuralist of Neo-Bloomfieldian school of American linguistics, while emphasizing empirical data, ignored and actually abstracted (Bailey, 1971) from the variation which is an integral part of the "empirical data" they were collecting. Bloomfield (1933), the founder of modern structuralism, for example, states that language changes, but it changes so slowly that we cannot observe the change. Bloomfield also observes that there is individual and dialect variation in language, but that linguistics should seek homogeneous data and descriptions.

> It is something of a paradox that the greatest degree of abstracting away from variation in the data has been advocated by empiricist linguists. Linguistic thought in the thirties and forties in America was dominated by a positivist philosophy of science and a behaviorist methodology. The empiricist-positivist orientation (derived ultimately from medieval nominalism but immediately from Romanticism) stressed the reality of the individual datum and was loath to admit the reality of abstractions. This outlook generally entails against reifying "natures" or other relations among single entities. Bloomfield was able to have his orientational cake and eat it too by attending to a particular set of homogeneous data as a means of abstracting away from the variation that is of course inherent in all language data.
> His thought was developed by his followers in such a way as to insist on abstracting not only from interpersonal differences, but even from the stylistic differences of a single speaker-hearer.
> (Bailey, 1971: 4-5).

The empiricist orientation of Bloomfield remained central to mainstream linguistic thought until 1957. In 1957, Chomsky questioned the basic language models of structural linguistics and proposed the first version of transformational grammar. Later developments by Chomsky and others resulted in the development of the Standard theory (Chomsky, 1965) of generative transformational linguistics and in a decidedly different orientation of linguistics to mentalism, rationalism, and cognitive psychology. However, as Bailey (1971: 6-7) points out, the different orientation, while it helped greatly in developing a general theory about language, did not exactly help linguists to change their ideas about variation in language.

The advent of Noam Chomsky represented a swing of the pendulum to the opposite orientation -- the idealist or rationalist orientation. Chomsky taught linguists how to make valid argument and what a theory is, in addition to making mentalistic abstractions mentionable and providing a receptive and enthusiastic framework for the discussion of language universals, which had already been undertaken by Jakobson and Joseph Greenberg. Together with Morris Halle, Chomsky even broadened the restrictions that limited the analysis of variation to complementary phonetic and morphic variants.... Chomsky's insistence that a grammar account for what speakers can be inferentially shown to know about their language actually provides the grounds for including transtylistic and transpersonal variation in a grammatical analysis. But the Platonic point of view is as hostile to studying the interrelations found in the variation or flux of empirical data as positivism is. So it came about that Chomsky strongly endorsed his predecessors' view of interstylistic and interpersonal variation, though for quite different reasons....

As Bailey (1971) later demonstrates, there has been some progress in dealing linguistically with certain aspects of language variation, e.g., Klima's (1964) "linking rules", Chomsky and Halle's (1968) "high and low level rules", Troike's (1969) "generative diphonemic rules", and Houston's (1970) "systematic performance".

Although mainstream linguistics has been slow to recognize the need to incorporate variation into linguistic theory, there is relatively strong evidence of a growing tendency of proponents of Generative Semantics to recognize this need. Lakoff (1968) is a good example of this tendency. "It was no doubt clear to George Lakoff (1968: 22) when he proposed hierarchial constrains on anaphora with transpersonal validity, that the grammarian must go beyond the process of adding up idiolects if he is to find the grammatical pattern of the English language" (Bailey, 1971: 10). But even though at least some of the proponents of Generative Semantics are proposing the inclusion of some variation in linguistic theory, the use of quantifiable data and statistical analysis seems still to be anathema to them.

3.2 Dialectology.

Even though the mainstream linguists have generally ignored variation in language, there was one peripheral group of linguists who did study variation, the dialectologists. American dialectologists were interested primarily in isolated regional variation and based their studies on previous European models like Gillieron and Edmont (1902-12) and others.

Although Kurath's Linguistic Atlas work (1939) was a major undertaking, Pickford's (1956) scathing criticism of American dialectology raised major questions about even attempting a dialect study on existing methodology.

> By their selectivity, the cartographical surveys would deny the extent of the spread of urbanization in America.
>
> The Atlas surveys are not constructed to examine American speech even geographically. Neither the findings of the geographic surveys nor the interpretation can be trusted.... We have tried to show that the surveys of the Linguistic Atlas of the United States and Canada and related studies are not on the highest level of scientific research. They lack significance, validity, and reliability. Even at the time of its launching, he project was not sensitive enough to the complexity of American speech (Pickford, 1956: 228-229).

Later studies in dialectology, e.g., McDavid (1948) attempted to include some social differences in dialectology, although these studies were certainly not based on any kind of rigorous sampling procedures or statistical analysis.

3.3 Sociolinguistics.

It is in the field of sociolinguistics that the incorporation of variation into theory (indeed the use of variation in language as a focal-pivotal point of the theory) has been accomplished.

Although language in culture and society has been studied for a long time, modern sociolinguistics is relatively new. Scholars interested in sociolinguistics come from a variety of sources: sociology, anthropology, mainstream linguistics, historical linguistics, creolist studies and dialectology. But all sociolinguists agree that existing theories about language are not adequate to explain the complex phenomena associated with language competence and use.

Variation Theory

Of course, no linguist has, I think taken issue with the practice of abstracting from random, extralinguistic variation like the coughing, sighing, and panting that a tape recorder would pick up in the raw data. All linguists presumably take it for granted that such *performance variations* lie beyond the scope of non-pathological investigations. The issue lies rather in the degree of abstraction which should be made above this level of *systematic phonetics*, i.e., what variation above this level must be included in a grammatical description as part of a linguistic system, and what may legitimately be relegated to accidental performance as outside the system (Bailey, 1971: 4).

Although sociolinguists are interested in language variation and language functions in society, there are three main branches of sociolinguistics, depending on the concerns and the principal interests of the sociolinguist (Labov, 1970b). These areas are (1) the sociology of language, (2) the ethnography of communication, and (3) linguistics. Sociologists such as Fishman (1968) are particularly interested in the sociology of language, basically the use of language to answer sociological questions. Anthropologists seem more interested in the wholistic approach of Hymes (1964, 1968) to language in a communication situation. And linguists are interested in using sociolinguistics to solve linguistic problems. As Bailey (1971) has shown, however, the approaches of the ethnography of communication and linguistic sociolinguistics have been rapidly approaching common ground. Possibly in the future these two branches will merge.

However, since this study is primarily concerned with the use of sociolinguistics to solve linguistic problems, namely the problem of variation of sign language in the United States, the treatment of sociolinguistic theory in this monograph will center primarily in the recent developments in linguistic sociolinguistics, i.e., the development of variation theory.

3.4 The Development of Variation Theory.

Although mainstream linguists had admitted to language change (historical linguistics) and language variation (dialectology), these areas were generally considered outside the field of proper linguistics. Besides the orientation problems previously mentioned in Bailey (1971), another reason for the ignoring of variation is that linguists did not think that language change was observable (it was too slow) and they did not think that language variation was that regular. Linguists felt they had no tools to study these phenomena as they were happening.

Earlier linguists can perhaps be excused for some of their beliefs about language variation and change. The excuse cannot extend so readily to later linguists. In 1965, Chomsky stated:

> Linguistic theory is concerned primarily with an ideal speaker-listener, in a completely homogeneous speech community, who knows its language perfectly and is unaffected by such grammatically irrelevant conditions as (performance variations). This seems to me to have been the position of the founders of modern general linguistics, and no cogent reason for modifying it has been offered (Chomsky 1965: 34).

However, in 1963, Labov had studied a non-homogeneous community and had demonstrated that variation that existed in the community was describable in linguistic terms. In the same paper, Labov argued that language change and language variation are closely connected. Language variation is an indication of language change. By studying variation through the use of statistical data, we can predict language change.

Labov primarily entered the study of sociolinguistics through interest in language change. Through this interest in the mechanisms of linguistic change, Labov was not only able to demonstrate that variation was a sign of linguistic change and that variation was linguistically describable, he was also able to demonstrate in 1966 that statistical measurement of language use could be correlated with social class. This supposes the fact that one can predict the direction (and place of incipience) of linguistic change as well as the actual change itself.

Later work by Wolfram (1969), Fasold (1970, 1972b) and others reinforced Labov's findings. The highpoint in this trend of linguistic sociolinguistics has been the creation and utilization of the variable rule.

3.4.1 The Variable Rule.

The variable rule is in actuality an optional linguistic rule that assigns a hierarchial rating to certain features of environments in the rule. This weighting is an indication of the relative percentages of occurrence. Labov's first treatise of the variable rule occurred in "Contraction, Deletion, and Inherent Variability of the English Copula"; it will be treated only in brief and theoretical terms in this monograph.

An example of a hypothetical variable rule follows:

$$X \rightarrow (\emptyset) / \alpha Y \underline{\qquad} \gamma W$$
$$\beta Z$$

This variable rule states that X becomes optionally deleted when it is preceded by Y and Z and followed by W. The rule further states that the feature marked α is the most heavily weighted feature, ß is the next most heavily weighted feature, and γ is the next most heavily weighted feature. The following chart shows the conditions underwhich the rule applies.

Table 4
FREQUENCY OF APPLICATION
OF THE HYPOTHETICAL VARIABLE RULE

α	β	γ	
+	+	+	The rule applies most frequently
+	+	−	The rule applies 2nd most frequently
+	−	+	The rule applies 3rd most frequently
+	−	−	The rule applies 4th most frequently
−	+	+	The rule applies 5th most frequently
−	+	−	The rule applies 6th most frequently
−	−	+	The rule applies 7th most frequently
−	−	−	The rule applies 8th most frequently

Labov (1969), Fasold (1970), and Wolfram (1972) have argued that variable rules are part of linguistic competence. Variable rules do not actually represent real percentages of occurrence but represent relative frequencies. Thus actual percentages or statistics are not part of a competence of a user of a language, but knowledge of relative percentages is. This view, as we shall see has been questioned by some other sociolinguists.

3.4.2 Implicational Analysis.

The other major approach to variation in language has been implicational analysis. A number of people associated with this type of analysis have been creolists at one time or another. This is an interesting situation, since creolists, like Labov, are interested in language change. However, the type of language change that creolists observe (that is through language variation) is much more widespread and more rapidly changeable than the type of variation that Labov, Fasold, Wolfram, and other like-minded sociolinguists have concentrated on. Whether this difference caused the difference in theoretical development is not known. In fact, there seems to have been no treatment of this possibility in linguistic literature.

Whatever the reason for the difference in theoretical development, a difference has developed. Stoltz and Bills (1968) and DeCamp (1968) both proposed early implicational models for the handling of variation. In an implicational model, there will be a set of features $\underline{A}$, $\underline{B}$, $\underline{C}$, $\underline{D}$, etc. that may be arranged in such an order that $\underline{A} \supset \underline{B} \supset \underline{C} \supset \underline{D}$. This means that if a lect (Some sociolinguists, e.g., Bailey (1971) have proposed the use of the word "lect" instead of "dialect" since a real dialect, a speech community bounded by isogloss bundles, is rarely found. Almost everyone uses a transitional dialect. To avoid the presumptions of the term "dialect", lect has been suggested as a substitute.) has $\underline{A}$, it will also have $\underline{B}$, $\underline{C}$, $\underline{D}$; if a lect does not have $\underline{A}$, but has $\underline{B}$, it will have $\underline{C}$, $\underline{D}$; and so on. Thus for a set of four features there are mathematically 16 possible lectal arrangements (2^4). However, most features and rules are implicationally ordered. If the features are implicationally ordered, there is only a possibility of five lects (4 + 1). Languages do not tend to have the mathematically possible number of lects; languages tend to have lects that can be described implicationally.

TABLE 5
POSSIBLE LECTS WITH FOUR FEATURES

	A	B	C	D
1	+	+	+	+
2	+	+	+	−
3	+	+	−	+
4	+	+	−	−
5	+	−	+	+
6	+	−	+	−
7	+	−	−	+
8	+	−	−	−
9	−	+	+	+
10	−	+	+	−
11	−	+	−	+
12	−	+	−	−
13	−	−	+	+
14	−	−	+	−
15	−	−	−	+
16	−	−	−	−

TABLE 6
POSSIBLE LECTS WITH FOUR FEATURES IN IMPLICATIONAL ORDER

	A	B	C	D
1	+	+	+	+
2	−	+	+	+
3	−	−	+	+
4	−	−	−	+
5	−	−	−	−

3.4.3 Criticisms of the Two Models.

Although the two models for handling variation both appeared about the same, the implicational analysis was the first to receive criticism. Fasold (1970) pointed out two problems with implicational analysis.

Since implicational analysis requires binary decisions (i.e., a given speaker or group of speakers either has or does not have a certain feature), and the data are apparently often variable, how can such binary decisions be made? The problem is discussed by Stoltz and Bills:

"A certain degree of arbitrariness is introduced into this use of scalogram analysis because of the requirement that each informant be given either a 1 or a 0 on each variable. Thus we cannot enter into the analysis each informant's proportion of usage of a given feature; he must be scored categorically on whether he uses the standard version of the feature or not. Since the data usually do not come in this all-or-nothing way, the necessity arose for setting a threshold for each feature." (Fasold, 1970: 552-3).

Stoltz and Bills later discussed the problem of setting a threshold. The problem is that their methodology seems too ad hoc. Fasold also questions the validity of choosing an arbitrary set of features to scale and mentions the problem that this earlier scalogram analysis did not take environment into consideration.

On the other hand, the variable rule is not without its critics. Bickerton (1971) has stated that he does not feel that variable rules can be part of the competence of a speaker (How can a speaker learn relative percentages of use?) and he feels that variable rules are not necessary in the type of poly-lectal and pan-lectal grammars that he wants to write.

However, although it appears that proponents of the two models for describing variation differ, the two models actually seem to be moving closer together (DeCamp, 1972). One impetus for this merging may be the idea of the wave model.

3.4.4 The Wave Model.

Bailey's (1970) wave model essentially proposes that language spreads in waves throughout a society. These waves may be represented by implicational scales. Thus the implicational scale shown in Table 6 is actually showing a historical change. A is the first part of the change B the second, and so forth.

Bailey (1970), Bickerton (1971), and Fasold (1970) have

suggested the use of variable features in implicational scales, instead of limiting oneself to only binary distinctions. Thus, table 7 states that there is variability wherever an x occurs. That is the change from 1̲ to 0̲ is not completed. (It should be noted that Fasold uses 1̲ for ±, x̲ for x, and 0̲ for −.)

TABLE 7
IMPLICATIONAL PATTERNS WITH VARIATION
(FASOLD, 1972a)

Lects	A	B	C	D
1	1	1	1	1
2	1	1	1	x
3	1	1	x	x
4	1	x	x	0
5	x	x	0	0
6	x	0	0	0
7	0	0	0	0

Bailey has also proposed the idea that the more heavily weighted features in variable rules are the earliest features in which the rule began to operate. Features marked α are the most heavily weighted environment, where the rule began to apply first; ß features are the next most heavily weighted features, where the rule next began to apply, etc. Therefore the application of the variable rule in environment γ implies application of the rule in environment ß, and the application of the variable rule in environment ß implies the application of the rule in environment α, another set of implications. In conjunction with Bailey's proposal, Fasold (1972a) has suggested that frequency patterns can be included in variable implications. Thus we may set up implications like Table 8 below, where N̲ indicates a greater frequency of occurrence than N and N indicates a greater frequency of occurrence than n and n indicates a greater frequency of occurrence than n.

TABLE 8
FREQUENCY PATTERN
(FASOLD, 1972a)

Lects	α	β	γ
1	1	N̲	N
2	N̲	N	n
3	N	n̲	n
4	n̲	n	0
5	n	0	0
6	0	0	0

Thus, it seems that the use of implicational scales and variable rules is, at least, partially approaching common ground, although there is still some debate on the necessity of including variable rules in grammars. Probably variable rules are needed for descriptions of some aspects of productive competence, though they probably are not needed to describe receptive competence, since even Labov (1970b) himself thinks that perception of variation may well be categorical. But whether variable rules are used in a grammar or not, there seems to be a definite trend in sociolinguistics towards a new kind of grammar.

3.4.5 Panlectal and Polylectal Grammars.

Bickerton (1971, 1972), Bailey (1971) and others feel that existing monolectal grammars, grammars of only one variety of a language, do not show insights into language that polylectal and panlectal grammars can.

> People who have envisaged grammars that would generate more than one variety of a language have done so in terms of a unitary core grammar with sets of additional rules (alternatives) at the end. This accords with the generative supposition that dialects of the same language will differ only in low-level rules (cf. Chomsky, 1964); one which can easily, if circularly, be reinforced by appropriate definitions of 'language' and 'dialect'. Unfortunately, no one has yet succeeded in deciding whether the varieties of language we shall be discussing here are 'dialects of English' or 'separate languages' (Guyanese Creole English) . . .. since, as I hope to show, some of these varieties differ from English at a relatively deep level, it is hard to see how a 'core-and-appendage' grammar could generate all of them (Bickerton, 1972: 4-5).

Given a language continuum situation, like the above example or the language situation in the deaf community, a linguist cannot isolate language varieties very easily. Thus it is impossible to describe the situation as code-switching, since the linguist hasn't yet defined the codes.

> It follows that a polylectal grammar will contain no 'switching' rules as such. It will have a series of rules similar in form to existing types of generative rules, but some of which will in effect be rewritings and re-rewritings of 'earlier' rules; in addition, it will contain a 'rule-shift component' which will specify the selection from the overall series required to generate each successive isolect
> (Bickerton, 1972: 10-11).

Bickerton goes on to state that, for a grammar of this type, he presupposes a universal set of semantic base rules and sets of semantic features that would trigger appropriate T-rules in the appropriate order to describe the points on the continuum that are within the competence of a given user of the language.

Thus a polylectal grammar or panlectal grammar describes more than the competence of any one user of the language. But the competences of all users of the language varieties are included in a panlectal grammar and are actually recoverable given the proper situational, social, and personal profile. A panlectal grammar then shows not only the proper relationships of rules in the competence of a given ideal speaker-listener (Chomsky, 1965) but also shows the relation between one given speaker's rules and another's in proper historical prospective. This far surpasses the descriptive and explanatory ability of any existing monolectal grammar.

3.5 Summary.

Until recently, language change and variation have not generally been optimally utilized by mainstream linguists. But actually language variation is a sign of linguistic change. Much variation is regular and predictable, and it is generally relatable with social factors. Variable rules, optional rules with weighted features, are one way of describing variation. Implicational patternings are another.

More heavily weighted features on variable rules implies earlier on an implicational scale and more frequent in occurrence in language production. Implicational scales are indications of a series of changes taking place in the language, and implications give clues to the proper hierarchial arrangement necessary to order and reorder the T-rules and phonological rules to write a polylectal or panlectal grammar.

Polylectal and panlectal grammars are more descriptively and explanatorily adequate than existing monolectal grammars and allow the linguist to demonstrate competence of a given user (and indeed of all users) of the language varieties along a language continuum without having to resort to a usually inadequate explanation of code-switching.

3.6 Conclusion.

Polylectal and panlectal grammars may lead to feasible and insightful ways of describing variation on language continuums. Since the deaf language situation is a diglossic continuum, it is felt that variable scaling, panlectal rules, and possibly variable rules are viable ways to approach the study of the American Sign Language to English continuum.

Chapter IV
Field Methods

4.1 Data Gathering.
The data on which this study is based were collected during the fall of 1972 in Washington, D. C., Frederick, Maryland, and New York City. The data were collected through the use of a videotape and a questionnaire.

4.1.1 Instruments.

4.1.1.1 The Videotape.
 Variation in Sign Language had been previously observed by the investigator in three grammatical areas: (1) Negation, (2) Agent-Beneficiary Directionality, and (3) Reduplication of Verbs. The tape consisted of six minutes of signing by a deaf informant with deaf parents who learned signs before the age of six and who finished college. On this tape she produced the noted variations in isolation. Her performance was shown to small groups of informants who were asked to indicate on a questionnaire form whether or not they ever use the signed form. The entire procedure generally took from twenty to thirty minutes.
 Labov (1970b), as well as most sociolinguists who prefer the variable rule approach to variation, normally record free conversation and then analyze the tapes for variation. However, as Labov (1970b) also points out, it is not always possible to obtain desired forms on tape in free conversation.
 One way to obtain these forms is through the intuitive re-

actions of the users of the language. Do they accept the forms or not? Do they say that they use the form or not? This approach using intuitive reactions is the procedure used in this study, since it was felt that most of the desired forms would not be obtained in free conversation. A will be seen later, the percentages of acceptability obtained on the data are well over the 85% level set by Guttman (1944) for valid implicational information.

Several words of caution should be issued, however. When one is dealing with stigmatized forms, he may very well encounter much difficulty using this approach, since many people are not willing to admit that they use such forms. However, the forms used in this study do not appear to be stigmatized. Thus no particular problems were encountered.

Every effort should also be made to look for the same variation in free conversation to test out the results obtained through mass intuition. This has been done informally by the investigator before and after the study. (It should be remembered that it was observed variation that led to the designing of the questionnaire to include forms that frequently varied.) However, further systematic observation also needs to be done. This further research is discussed in Chapter 8.

4.1.1.2 The Questionnaire.

The questionnaire is divided into two parts: background information and responses. The original questionnaire was modified slightly during the study. The background information section remained the same; the response section was shortened. There were two reasons for this: (1) the extra question on each response was not easy for many informants to answer probably because it was too hypothetical; (2) the extra question on each response almost doubled the time required to complete the test.

Copies of the original and the modified questionnaires are included on the following pages.

Field Methods

BACKGROUND INFORMATION

Number _____

1. Age: _____ 2. Sex: _____ 3. Race: _____

4. Education (Circle the grade completed)
   1 2 3 4 5 6 7 8 9 10 11 12   1 2 3 4   1 2 3 4
                                  college   grad. school

5. Occupation: _____

6. Do you consider yourself: (Circle one)
   a. hearing   b. hard of hearing   c. deaf

7. If you have a hearing loss, how old were you when your hearing loss occurred? _____

8. Does any member of your family have a hearing loss?
   a. No
   b. Father c. Mother d. sister e. brother f. Other _____

9. What is your first language? _____

10. Which of the following do you prefer? (Circle one)
    a. American Sign Language   b. Signed English
    c. Simultaneous Communication   d. Speech
    e. Home Signs   f. Rochester Method

11. How old were you when you learned how to sign? _____

12. Are most of your friends:
    a. hearing   b. hard of hearing   c. deaf

13. Father's occupation: _____

14. Mother's occupation: _____

15. Father's education: (Circle the grade completed)
    1 2 3 4 5 6 7 8 9 10 11 12   1 2 3 4   1 2 3 4
                                   college   grad. school

16. Mother's education: (Circle the grade completed)
    1 2 3 4 5 6 7 8 9 10 11 12   1 2 3 4   1 2 3 4
                                   college   grad. school

17. Father's first language: _____

18. Mother's first language: _____

RESPONSES (ORIGINAL QUESTIONNAIRE)

Part I
1a.   Do you use this for "don't know" (Circle one)
       a. yes   b. probably yes   c. probably no   d. no

If you use this, do you use it with: (Circle as many as you like)
    a. hearing people -- good signers
    b. hearing people -- bad signers
    c. educated deaf people
    d. uneducated deaf people

1b.   Do you use this for "don't know"
       a. yes   b. probably yes   c. probably no   d. no

If you use this, do you use it with: (Circle as many as you like)
    a. hearing people -- good signers
    b. hearing people -- bad signers
    c. educated deaf people
    d. uneducated deaf people

2a.   Do you use this for "don't want"
       a. yes   b. probably yes   c. probably no   d. no

If you use this, do you use it with: (Circle as many as you like)
    a. hearing people -- good signers
    b. hearing people -- bad signers
    c. educated deaf people
    d. uneducated deaf people

2b.   Do you use this for "don't want"
       a. yes   b. probably yes   c. probably no   d. no

If you use this, do you use it with: (Circle as many as you like)
    a. hearing people -- good signers
    b. hearing people -- bad signers
    c. educated deaf people
    d. uneducated deaf people

3a.   Do you use this for "bad"
       a. yes   b. probably yes   c. probably no   d. no

If you use this, do you use it with: (Circle as many as you like)
    a. hearing people -- good signers
    b. hearing people -- bad signers
    c. educated deaf people
    d. uneducated deaf people

Field Methods

3b. Do you use this for "bad"
    a. yes   b. probably yes   c. probably no   d. no

If you use this, do you use it with: (Circle as many as you like)
    a. hearing people -- good signers
    b. hearing people -- bad signers
    c. educated deaf people
    d. uneducated deaf people

4a. Do you use this for "don't like"
    a. yes   b. probably yes   c. probably no   d. no

If you use this, do you use it with: (Circle as many as you like)
    a. hearing people -- good signers
    b. hearing people -- bad signers
    c. educated deaf people
    d. uneducated deaf people

4b. Do you use this for "don't like"
    a. yes   b. probably yes   c. probably no   d. no

If you use this, do you use it with: (Circle as many as you like)
    a. hearing people -- good signers
    b. hearing people -- bad signers
    c. educated deaf people
    d. uneducated deaf people

5a. Do you use this for "don't have"
    a. yes   b. probably yes   c. probably no   d. no

If you use this, do you use it with: (Circle as many as you like)
    a. hearing people -- good signers
    b. hearing people -- bad signers
    c. educated deaf people
    d. uneducated deaf people

5b. Do you use this for "don't have"
    a. yes   b. probably yes   c. probably no   d. no

If you use this, do you use it with: (Circle as many as you like)
    a. hearing people -- good signers
    b. hearing people -- bad signers
    c. educated deaf people
    d. uneducated deaf people

Part II

1a. Do you use this for "you give me"
    a. yes   b. probably yes   c. probably no   d. no

If you use this, do you use it with: (Circle as many as you like)
    a. hearing people -- good signers
    b. hearing people -- bad signers
    c. educated deaf people
    d. uneducated deaf people

1b. Do you use this for "you give me"
    a. yes   b. probably yes   c. probably no   d. no

If you use this, do you use it with: (Circle as many as you like)
    a. hearing people -- good signers
    b. hearing people -- bad signers
    c. educated deaf people
    d. uneducated deaf people

2a. Do you use this for "you ask me"
    a. yes   b. probably yes   c. probably no   d. no

If you use this, do you use it with: (Circle as many as you like)
    a. hearing people -- good signers
    b. hearing people -- bad signers
    c. educated deaf people
    d. uneducated deaf people

2b. Do you use this for "you ask me"
    a. yes   b. probably yes   c. probably no   d. no

If you use this, do you use it with: (Circle as many as you like)
    a. hearing people -- good signers
    b. hearing people -- bad signers
    c. educated deaf people
    d. uneducated deaf people

3a. Do you use this for "you show me"
    a. yes   b. probably yes   c. probably no   d. no

If you use this, do you use it with: (Circle as many as you like)
    a. hearing people -- good signers
    b. hearing people -- bad signers
    c. educated deaf people
    d. uneducated deaf people

3b.   Do you use this for "you show me"
         a. yes   b. probably yes   c. probably no   d. no

If you use this, do you use it with: (Circle as many as you like)
         a. hearing people -- good signers
         b. hearing people -- bad signers
         c. educated deaf people
         d. uneducated deaf people

4a.   Do you use this for "you hate me"
         a. yes   b. probably yes   c. probably no   d. no

If you use this, do you use it with: (Circle as many as you like)
         a. hearing people -- good signers
         b. hearing people -- bad signers
         c. educated deaf people
         d. uneducated deaf people

4b.   Do you use this for "you hate me"
         a. yes   b. probably yes   c. probably no   d. no

If you use this, do you use it with: (Circle as many as you like)
         a. hearing people -- good signers
         b. hearing people -- bad signers
         c. educated deaf people
         d. uneducated deaf people

5a.   Do you use this for "you hit me"
         a. yes   b. probably yes   c. probably no   d. no

If you use this, do you use it with: (Circle as many as you like)
         a. hearing people -- good signers
         b. hearing people -- bad signers
         c. educated deaf people
         d. uneducated deaf people

5b.   Do you use this for "you hit me"
         a. yes   b. probably yes   c. probably no   d. no

If you use this, do you use it with: (Circle as many as you like)
         a. hearing people -- good signers
         b. hearing people -- bad signers
         c. educated deaf people
         d. uneducated deaf people

6a.   Do you use this for "you tell me"
        a. yes   b. probably yes   c. probably no   d. no

If you use this, do you use it with: (Circle as many as you like)
        a. hearing people -- good signers
        b. hearing people -- bad signers
        c. educated deaf people
        d. uneducated deaf people

6b.   Do you use this for "you tell me"
        a. yes   b. probably yes   c. probably no   d. no

If you use this, do you use it with: (Circle as many as you like)
        a. hearing people -- good signers
        b. hearing people -- bad signers
        c. educated deaf people
        d. uneducated deaf people

7a.   Do you use this for "you force me"
        a. yes   b. probably yes   c. probably no   d. no

If you use this, do you use it with: (Circle as many as you like)
        a. hearing people -- good signers
        b. hearing people -- bad signers
        c. educated deaf people
        d. uneducated deaf people

7b.   Do you use this for "you force me"
        a. yes   b. probably yes   c. probably no   d. no

If you use this, do you use it with: (Circle as many as you like)
        a. hearing people -- good signers
        b. hearing people -- bad signers
        c. educated deaf people
        d. uneducated deaf people

8a.   Do you use this for "you fingerspell to me"
        a. yes   b. probably yes   c. probably no   d. no

If you use this, do you use it with: (Circle as many as you like)
        a. hearing people -- good signers
        b. hearing people -- bad signers
        c. educated deaf people
        d. uneducated deaf people

Field Methods	39

8b.	Do you use this for "you fingerspell to me"
	a. yes b. probably yes c. probably no d. no

If you use this, do you use it with: (Circle as many as you like)
    a. hearing people -- good signers
    b. hearing people -- bad signers
    c. educated deaf people
    d. uneducated deaf people

9a.	Do you use this for "you say no to me"
	a. yes b. probably yes c. probably no d. no

If you use this, do you use it with: (Circle as many as you like)
    a. hearing people -- good signers
    b. hearing people -- bad signers
    c. educated deaf people
    d. uneducated deaf people

9b.	Do you use this for "you say no to me"
	a. yes b. probably yes c. probably no d. no

If you use this, do you use it with: (Circle as many as you like)
    a. hearing people -- good signers
    b. hearing people -- bad signers
    c. educated deaf people
    d. uneducated deaf people

Part III

1a.	Do you use this way of signing "read"
	a. yes b. probably yes c. probably no d. no

If you use this, do you use it with: (Circle as many as you like)
    a. hearing people -- good signers
    b. hearing people -- bad signers
    c. educated deaf people
    d. uneducated deaf people

2.	Do you use this way of signing "want"
	a. yes b. probably yes c. probably no d. no

If you use this, do you use it with: (Circle as many as you like)
    a. hearing people -- good signers
    b. hearing people -- bad signers
    c. educated deaf people
    d. uneducated deaf people

3. Do you use this way of signing "drive"
    a. yes   b. probably yes   c. probably no   d. no

If you use this, do you use it with: (Circle as many as you like)
    a. hearing people -- good signers
    b. hearing people -- bad signers
    c. educated deaf people
    d. uneducated deaf people

4. Do you use this way of signing "memorize"
    a. yes   b. probably yes   c. probably no   d. no

If you use this, do you use it with: (Circle as many as you like)
    a. hearing people -- good signers
    b. hearing people -- bad signers
    c. educated deaf people
    d. uneducated deaf people

5. Do you use this way of signing "study"
    a. yes   b. probably yes   c. probably no   d. no

If you use this, do you use it with: (Circle as many as you like)
    a. hearing people -- good signers
    b. hearing people -- bad signers
    c. educated deaf people
    d. uneducated deaf people

6. Do you use this way of signing "see"
    a. yes   b. probably yes   c. probably no   d. no

If you use this, do you use it with: (Circle as many as you like)
    a. hearing people -- good signers
    b. hearing people -- bad signers
    c. educated deaf people
    d. uneducated deaf people

7. Do you use this way of signing "run"
    a. yes   b. probably yes   c. probably no   d. no

If you use this, do you use it with: (Circle as many as you like)
    a. hearing people -- good signers
    b. hearing people -- bad signers
    c. educated deaf people
    d. uneducated deaf people

Field Methods 41

8. Do you use this way of signing "know"
    a. yes   b. probably yes   c. probably no   d. no

If you use this, do you use it with: (Circle as many as you like)
    a. hearing people -- good signers
    b. hearing people -- bad signers
    c. educated deaf people
    d. uneducated deaf people

9. Do you use this way of signing "meet"
    a. yes   b. probably yes   c. probably no   d. no

If you use this, do you use it with: (Circle as many as you like)
    a. hearing people -- good signers
    b. hearing people -- bad signers
    c. educated deaf people
    d. uneducated deaf people

RESPONSES (MODIFIED QUESTIONNAIRE)
Part I
1a. Do you use this for "don't know" (Circle one)
     a. yes   b. probably yes   c. probably no   d. no
1b. Do you use this for "don't know"
     a. yes   b. probably yes   c. probably no   d. no
2a. Do you use this for "don't want"
     a. yes   b. probably yes   c. probably no   d. no
2b. Do you use this for "don't want"
     a. yes   b. probably yes   c. probably no   d. no
3a. Do you use this for "bad"
     a. yes   b. probably yes   c. probably no   d. no
3b. Do you use this for "bad"
     a. yes   b. probably yes   c. probably no   d. no
4a. Do you use this for "don't like"
     a. yes   b. probably yes   c. probably no   d. no
4b. Do you use this for "don't like"
     a. yes   b. probably yes   c. probably no   d. no
5a. Do you use this for "don't have"
     a. yes   b. probably yes   c. probably no   d. no
5b. Do you use this for "don't have"
     a. yes   b. probably yes   c. probably no   d. no

Part II
1a. Do you use this for "you give me"
     a. yes   b. probably yes   c. probably no   d. no
1b. Do you use this for "you give me"
     a. yes   b. probably yes   c. probably no   d. no
2a. Do you use this for "you ask me"
     a. yes   b. probably yes   c. probably no   d. no
2b. Do you use this for "you ask me"
     a. yes   b. probably yes   c. probably no   d. no

3a. Do you use this for "you show me"
   a. yes   b. probably yes   c. probably no   d. no
3b. Do you use this for "you show me"
   a. yes   b. probably yes   c. probably no   d. no
4a. Do you use this for "you hate me"
   a. yes   b. probably yes   c. probably no   d. no
4b. Do you use this for "you hate me"
   a. yes   b. probably yes   c. probably no   d. no
5a. Do you use this for "you hit me"
   a. yes   b. probably yes   c. probably no   d. no
5b. Do you use this for "you hit me"
   a. yes   b. probably yes   c. probably no   d. no
6a. Do you use this for "you tell me"
   a. yes   b. probably yes   c. probably no   d. no
6b. Do you use this for "you tell me"
   a. yes   b. probably yes   c. probably no   d. no
7a. Do you use this for "you force me"
   a. yes   b. probably yes   c. probably no   d. no
7b. Do you use this for "you force me"
   a. yes   b. probably yes   c. probably no   d. no
8a. Do you use this for "you fingerspell to me"
   a. yes   b. probably yes   c. probably no   d. no
8b. Do you use this for "you fingerspell to me"
   a. yes   b. probably yes   c. probably no   d. no
9a. Do you use this for "you say no to me"
   a. yes   b. probably yes   c. probably no   d. no
9b. Do you use this for "you say no to me"
   a. yes   b. probably yes   c. probably no   d. no

Part III
1. Do you use this way of signing "read"
   a. yes   b. probably yes   c. probably no   d. no
2. Do you use this way of signing "want"
   a. yes   b. probably yes   c. probably no   d. no
3. Do you use this way of signing "drive"
   a. yes   b. probably yes   c. probably no   d. no
4. Do you use this way of signing "memorize"
   a. yes   b. probably yes   c. probably no   d. no
5. Do you use this way of signing "study"
   a. yes   b. probably yes   c. probably no   d. no
6. Do you use this way of signing "see"
   a. yes   b. probably yes   c. probably no   d. no
7. Do you use this way of signing "run"
   a. yes   b. probably yes   c. probably no   d. no
8. Do you use this way of signing "know"
   a. yes   b. probably yes   c. probably no   d. no
9. Do you use this way of signing "meet"
   a. yes   b. probably yes   c. probably no   d. no

4.1.2 Informants.

One hundred and forty-one informants were used in this study. These informants vary in age from 13 to 55. Younger children were not included in the study since child language acquisition factors might be operating in the responses and, as Fasold (1972b) points out, children are not as adept at noticing social differences in language.

There were 63 males and 73 females in the study, while 5 did not indicate their sex. The majority of informants were White with only 9 Blacks included in the study. 7 informants did not indicate their race. Black signers followed the same implicational patterns as Whites in the linguistic variables used in this study. However, recent preliminary research in Atlanta (Woodward and Erting, 1973) and in New Orleans (Donnels, 1973, and La. R.I.D., 1973) indicates that Southern Black signing appears to be very different from Southern White signing and Northern Black and White signing. Further research is needed to describe these differences systematically.

Most sociolinguists have attempted to relate social class with linguistic variation. They have generally assumed that social class may be described by an inter-relation of education, occupation, and income. Other social factors such as age and sex also have been shown to be related with linguistic variation (Wolfram, 1969, and Trudgill, 1972).

It was felt that for this study of the deaf, four social variables might correlate well with variation in sign language. These variables are whether a person is ± deaf, has ± deaf parents, learned signs ± before the age of six, and has ± attended some college. Table 9 shows the classification of informants by these social variables.

TABLE 9
CLASSIFICATION OF INFORMANTS
BY SOCIAL VARIABLES

Number	Deaf	Deaf Parents	Before six	College
14	+	+	+	+
13	+	+	+	−
0*	+	+	−	+
0*	+	+	−	−
12	+	−	+	+
17	+	−	+	−
18	+	−	−	+
34	+	−	−	−
8	−	+	+	+
0*	−	+	+	−
0*	−	+	−	+
0*	−	+	−	−
1*	−	−	+	+
0*	−	−	+	−
24	−	−	−	+
0*	−	−	−	−

*These groups contain very small memberships and are extremely difficult to find.

Basically there are two reasons for choosing these four variables over others. (1) the investigator did not feel it was justified to assume social class was determined in the same way for both the hearing and the deaf communities. (2) It seems that the first three of these social variables are extremely important criteria for socialization into the deaf community. Very few hearing people can really be considered part of the deaf community. As mentioned earlier, Meadow (1972) points out that socialization into the deaf community invariably includes language socialization. With the children of deaf parents this language socialization generally takes place at birth. With children of hearing parents it may take place at other times. However, the age of six seems to be a crucial time in first language acquisition. Quite possibly a person learning signs after the age of six will sign differently than a person who learned signs earlier.

The fourth variable, education, seems to be a universal social variable for those societies having a formal education system, since education tends to preserve and transmit traditional values toward language and society as well as to promote maintenance of language forms and structures that may not be present in everyday conversation.

4.2 Procedure.

Responses to the questionnaire were tabulated and implicational patterns were sought. Responses of "probably yes" were counted as "yes"; responses of "probably no" were counted as "no". There was also an attempt to relate linguistic variation with the four social variables. Since the number of informants in each lect was sometimes too small for a x-square test, the tests were run on halves of the implicational scales. Finally the information supplied by each implication was incorporated into the grammar by means of a rule that used weighted features.

Results of the analysis are discussed in the remaining chapters.

Chapter V
Variation in Negation

5.1 Negative Incorporation.

5.1.1 Negative Incorporation Implication.

American Sign Language has several verbs that may be negated by a bound outward twisting movement from the place where the sign is made. Bergman (1972) mentions polarity (which includes Negative Incorporation as it is used here), however, he makes no linguistic analysis of this structure. The derivational history of an example of Negative Incorporation is described below.

1.

    $\cap B_T \times \underset{\perp}{\triangledown}$ $[] G_T \times$

    NOT   ME
    KNOW

    "I don't know."

The underlying structure for this sentence is represented in 1a. on the following page.

1a.*

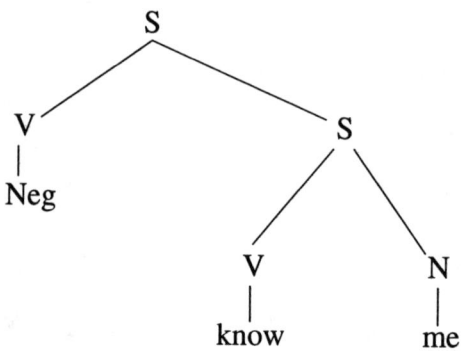

Predicate lowering results in 1b.

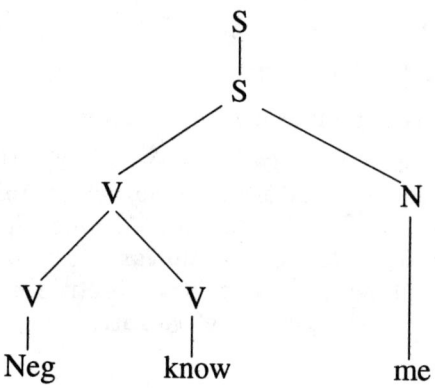

A pruning rule allows us to delete the highest S node yielding yielding 1c on the following page.

---

*Only essential structures are listed in trees in this paper. 1a. probably needs an underlying object that is later deleted. However, since this object is not essential to the tree in question, it is not included.

1c.
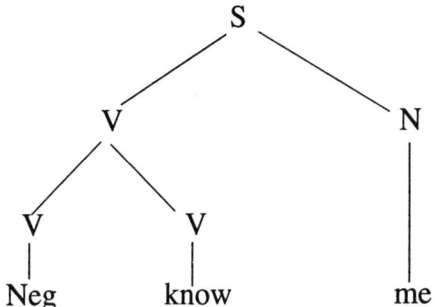

Negative incorporation then yields

1d.
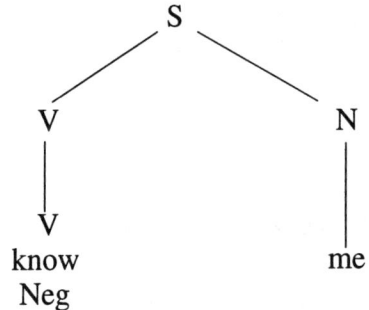

A final pruning rule gives

1e.
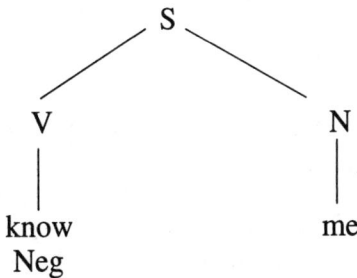

Later rules would give a surface structure symbolization to the lexical units and rewrite Neg here as an outward movement of the dez from the tab with a twist of the hand.

Not all verbs undergo Negative Incorporation. Five verbs that undergo this transformation were used in this study:

∩ B_T ˣ	C_a C_a ᵀ·	∪ B_T ⊥	[]5< #[8]	[]ᐧᐧᐧᐧᐧ ˣ
KNOW	WANT	GOOD	LIKE	HAVE

Before this study was begun, it was noticed that not every one who signs or who claims to use American Sign Language uses Negative Incorporation with all these verbs. There was considerable variation. The results of the questionnaire indicate this variation is implicational. The ordering for the implication is: "have" ⊃ "like" ⊃ "want" ⊃ "know" ⊃ "good". Based on this implicational ordering we have the six possible lects, shown in Table 10.

TABLE 10
IMPLICATIONAL LECTS FOR
NEGATIVE INCORPORATION

Lects	"have"	"like"	"want"	"know"	"good"
1	+	+	+	+	+
2	−	+	+	+	+
3	−	−	+	+	+
4	−	−	−	+	+
5	−	−	−	−	+
6	−	−	−	−	−

For this implicational scale to be valid, at least 85% (Guttman, 1944) of the responses, and preferably 89-90% (Bailey, 1973) of the responses must follow the implication in Table 10. With 141 informants and five slots for each person, the total number of responses numbered 705. There were 21 exceptions (listed in the Appendix) to the implicational scale, which is a 3% rate of exception or a 97% rate of following the implication

TABLE 11
MEMBERSHIP IN NEGATIVE INCORPORATION LECTS

Groups	+D +DP +B6 +C	+D +DP +B6 −C	+D −DP +B6 +C	+D −DP +B6 −C	+D −DP −B6 +C	+D −DP −B6 −C	−D +DP +B6 +C	−D −DP −B6 +C	Totals
Deaf									
Deaf Parents									
Before six									
College									
Lects									
1	1	4	1	2	2	7	2	2	21
2	3	4	3	2	5	6	1	4	28
3	8	5	5	8	10	14	4	5	59
4	2	0	3	2	1	2	1	11	22
5	0	0	0	3	0	5	1	2	11
6	0	0	0	0	0	0	0	0	0
Totals	14	13	12	17	18	34	9	24	141

—well over what is needed for a valid implication.

The information supplied by the implication must be incorporated into the grammar. Methodology for doing this will be discussed after the following discussion of the relation of these lects with social variables.

5.1.2 Relation of Negative Incorporation Lects with Social Variables.

Table 11 on page 51 shows the distribution in Negative Incorporation lects 1-6 according to grouping based on the four social variables of the study.

It is also possible to look at membership in the lects with relationship to each of the social variables. Tables 12-15 show the relationships.

TABLE 12a
MEMBERSHIP IN NEGATIVE INCORPORATION LECTS BASED ON DEAFNESS

Lects	+Deaf	-Deaf	Totals
1	17	4	21
2	23	5	28
3	50	9	59
4	10	12	22
5	8	3	11
6	0	0	0
Totals	108	33	141

Lects 1-3 comprise the half of the implicational scale that approaches "pure" American Sign Language Structure more closely, that is the half of the implicational scale that accepts Negative Incorporation in the most environments. Setting up a 2 by 2 chart, we can test significance of the variable ± deaf and membership in Negative Incorporation lects.

TABLE 12b
A 2 BY 2 REPRESENTATION OF TABLE 12a

Lects	+Deaf	-Deaf
1-3	90 (83%)	18 (55%)
4-6	18 (17%)	15 (45%)

A x-square test of this data shows a very strong dependency relationship (to the .005 level) of ±deaf and membership in Negative Incorporation lects. One is more likely to find a deaf person in lects 1-5 (closer to ASL) and more likely to find a hearing person in lects 6-10 (further from ASL).

TABLE 13a
MEMBERSHIP IN NEGATIVE INCORPORATION LECTS BASED ON PARENTAGE

Lects	+Deaf Parents	-Deaf Parents	Totals
1	7	14	21
2	8	20	28
3	17	42	59
4	3	19	22
5	1	10	11
6	0	0	0
Totals	36	105	141

TABLE 13b
A 2 BY 2 REPRESENTATION OF TABLE 13a

Lects	+Deaf Parents	-Deaf Parents
1-3	32 (89%)	76 (72%)
4-6	4 (11%)	29 (28%)

A x-square test shows no relationship between the social variable ± deaf parents and membership in Negative Incorporation lects.

TABLE 14a
MEMBERSHIP IN NEGATIVE INCORPORATION LECTS BASED ON AGE OF SIGN LANGUAGE ACQUISITION

Lects	+Before 6	-Before 6	Totals
1	10	11	21
2	13	15	28
3	30	29	59
4	8	14	22
5	4	7	11
6	0	0	0
Totals	65	76	141

TABLE 14b
A 2 BY 2 REPRESENTATION OF TABLE 14a

Lects	+Before 6	-Before 6
1-3	58 (82%)	55 (72%)
4-6	12 (18%)	21 (28%)

A x-square test shows no relationship between the social variable ±before six and membership in Negative Incorporation lects.

TABLE 15a
MEMBERSHIP IN NEGATIVE INCORPORATION LECTS BASED ON EDUCATION*

Lects	+College	-College	Totals
1	4	13	17
2	11	12	23
3	23	27	50
4	6	4	10
5	0	8	8
6	0	0	0
Totals	44	64	108

*Hearing informants are not included in this chart.

Variation in Negation

TABLE 15b
A 2 BY 2 REPRESENTATION OF TABLE 15a

Lects	+College	-College
1-3	38 (86%)	52 (81%)
4-6	6 (14%)	12 (19%)

A x-square test shows no relationship between education and membership in Negative Incorporation lects.

From Charts 12-15, we can state that membership in Negative Incorporation lects is related to the variable ±deaf and does not seem to be related to the variables of parentage, age of acquisition, and education. As intuitively expected, deaf informants fell into lects that were closer to ASL, although it is surprising that none of the other variables were significant. Other variables could also possibly be related to the membership in these lects.

5.1.3 Negative Incorporation Rule.

As discussed in Chapter 3, variation that may be described implicationally is language change in progress. The right end of the implicational scale shows the environments in which the rule applies first (the heaviest weighted environment). As we look towards the left of the implicational scale we see the successively later historical environments in which the rule applies.

Thus for the implication represented in Table 10, we saw that the Negative Incorporation rule applies for signers first in the environment of "good", second in the environment of "know", third in the environment of "want", fourth in the environment of "like", and fifth in the environment of "have".

Since this rule is undergoing historical change (both psycholinguistically and sociolinguistically), we presume that there are probably cherological and/or semantic features that are similar in these five verbs. It is possible to describe these five verbs in terms of cherological features. Table 16a shows the features necessary to distinguish these verbs.

TABLE 16a
FEATURES ON NEGATIVE INCORPORATION VERBS

Feature	have	like	want	know	good
appendage	−apd	−apd	−apd	+apd	+apd
body	+body	+body	−body	+body	+body
out sig	−out	+out	−out	−out	+out

From Table 16a we see that it is possible to weight these features assigning α to that feature that influences operation of the rule more frequently and that is the first environment historically in which the rule applies. To successfully less frequent environmental features we can assign, ß, γ etc. Table 16b shows the proper weighting of features.

TABLE 16b
WEIGHTED FEATURES ON
NEGATIVE INCORPORATION VERBS

"have"	"like"	"want"	"know"	"good"
			α apd	α apd
		β−body		
	γ out			γ out

The rule for Negative Incorporation which changed tree 1c to 1d can now be written.

Variation in Negation 57

```
[ [ NEG V        ] N ]
  s  v  +neg inc. v  s
         α apd
         β -body
         γ out

        1 2 3 4 5 6 7 ⇒
        1 2 4 5 6 7
        +out
        +twist
```

5.2 Not Negation.

5.2.1 Not Negation Implication.

The other type of variation in negation to be studied in Not Negation -- that is the negation of a verb by the negative sign $\cup \dot{A}^{\perp}$ "not". This seems to be a less formal sign than $\emptyset \, B_D{}^{\bullet} B_D \div$ "not (formal)". There m ay also be other differences between these "nots", however only variation in the informal "not" will be dealt with in this paper.

"Informal not" is used in American Sign Language as well as some varieties of Sign English and Manual English, but when "not" is used with verbs that may take Negative Incorporation, the resulting structure is definitely more toward the English part of the continuum. Thus while Negative Incorporation dealt with more American Sign Language Structure, Not Negation will deal with more Sign English structure. Following is a sample derivational history for an example of Not Negation Sign English structure.

2.

     [] I $^{\times}$ $\cup \dot{A}^{\perp}$ $\cap B_T{}^{\times}$

      I   NOT   KNOW

          "I don't know"

As seen below, the underlying structure for this sentence is the same as 1a.

2a. (1a.)

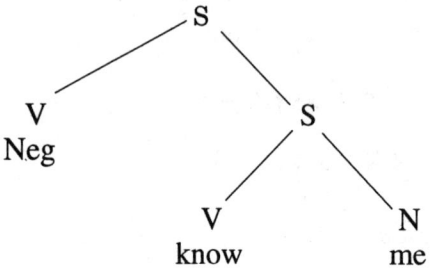

By predicate lowering, 2b is obtained.

2b. (1b.)

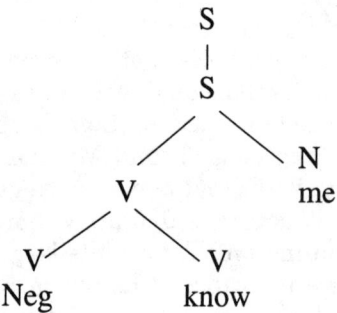

Tree pruning allows us to delete the highest S mode, yielding 2c.

2c. (1c.)

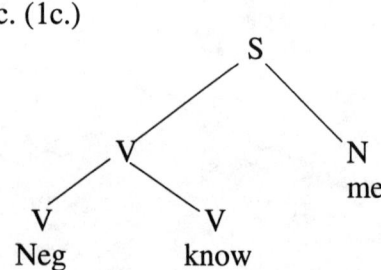

At this point in the derivation in example 1 we saw that the Negative Incorporation rule occurs. However, in a grammar more like Sign English, Negative Incorporation may be blocked for the verbs that may take Negative Incorporation. Thus a Sign English grammar will give a surface structure symbolization to each of the lexical units and will assign proper tense, case, and other rules.

Negative Incorporation is not always blocked for all verbs that may undergo Negative Incorporation. There is variation in Not Negation and this variation is implicational. The implicational scale for Not Negation is exactly the opposite of Negative Incorporation. Table 17 shows the implicational scale for Not Negation.

TABLE 17
IMPLICATIONAL LECTS FOR NOT NEGATION

Lects	"good"	"know"	"want"	"like"	"have"
1	+	+	+	+	+
2	–	+	+	+	+
3	–	–	+	+	+
4	–	–	–	+	+
5	–	–	–	–	+
6	–	–	–	–	–

This discussion of the Not Negation implication may seem a bit tautological to those familiar with implicational analysis. The Not Negation implication is exactly the mirror image of the Negative Incorporation implication. However, in this study we are dealing not only with inherent variability but also with *bilingual* competence. As we will see in Chapter 6, the mirror image of an implication will not always occur in true bilingual competence.

To my knowledge, this non-occurrence of a mirror image implication has not been encountered, let alone discussed before in implicational studies. DeCamp's (1963) and Bickerton's (1971, 1972) treatments of creoles do not discuss this situation. Perhaps this can be taken as evidence that the creole continuums they are discussing contain only one language. (Bickerton

TABLE 18
MEMBERSHIP IN NOT NEGATION LECTS

Groups	+D	+D	+D	+D	+D	+D	−D	−D	Totals
Deaf	+DP	+DP	−DP	−DP	−DP	−DP	+DP	−DP	
Deaf Parents	+B6	+B6	+B6	+B6	−B6	−B6	+B6	−B6	
Before six	+C	−C	+C	−C	+C	−C	+C	+C	
College									
Lects									
1	3	8	2	8	3	11	4	0	39
2	8	2	9	7	9	12	3	8	58
3	2	2	0	0	0	2	1	7	14
4	1	0	1	2	6	5	0	6	21
5	0	0	0	0	0	0	1	1	2
6	0	1	0	0	0	4	0	2	7
Totals	14	13	12	17	18	34	9	24	141

(1972) points out that no one knows whether the continuum he is describing contains one language or two.) Whether the non-occurrence of a mirror image implication is in actuality a sign that there are actually two languages contained in a continuum is not known. Certainly it would be interesting and useful if this were true, since the boundaries between one language and another are often hazy. Further research in this problem is urgently needed.

With 141 informants and five responses for each person for Not Negation, the total number of responses is 705. There were 31 exceptions (listed in the Appendix) to the implicational scale, which is a 4.4% rate of exception or a 95.8% rate of acceptability -- a strongly valid implication.

5.2.2 Relation of Not Negation Lects with Social Variables.

Table 18 shows the distribution of Not Negation lects 1-6 according to grouping based on the four social variables of this study.

It is possible to look at membership in the lects with relationship to each of the social variables. Charts 19-22 show the relationships.

TABLE 19a
MEMBERSHIP IN NOT NEGATION LECTS
BASED ON DEAFNESS

Lects	+Deaf	-Deaf	Totals
1	35	4	39
2	47	11	58
3	6	8	14
4	15	6	21
5	0	2	2
6	5	2	7
Totals	108	33	141

Lects 1-3 comprise the half of the implicational scale that approaches "pure" Sign English more closely, that is the half of the implicational scale that uses Not Negation in most environments. Setting up a 2 by 2 chart, we can test significance of the variable ±deaf and membership in Not Negation lects.

TABLE 19b
A 2 BY 2 REPRESENTATION OF TABLE 19a

Lects	+Deaf	-Deaf	Lects	+Deaf	-Deaf
1-3	88 (81%)	23 (70%)	1-2	82 (76%)	15 (45%)
4-6	20 (19%)	10 (30%)	3-6	26 (24%)	18 (55%)

The x-square tests of this data show no dependency relationship between membership in lects 1-3 and 4-6 and the social variable of ±deaf, but a very strong dependency relationship between membership in lects 1-2 and 3-6 and the variable ±deaf (to the .005 level). One is more likely to find a deaf person in lects 1-2 and more likely to find a hearing person in lects 3-6.

TABLE 20a
MEMBERSHIP IN NOT NEGATION LECTS
BASED ON PARENTAGE

Lects	+Deaf Parents	-Deaf Parents	Totals
1	15	24	39
2	13	45	58
3	6	8	14
4	1	20	21
5	1	1	2
6	0	7	7
Totals	36	105	141

TABLE 20b
A 2 BY 2 REPRESENTATION OF TABLE 20a

Lects	+Deaf Parents	-Deaf Parents
1-3	34 (94%)	77 (73%)
4-6	2 (6%)	28 (27%)

A x-square test shows a dependency relationship (.05 level) of ±deaf parents and membership in Not Negation lects. One is more likely to find a person with deaf parents in lects 1-3 and more likely to find a person with hearing parents in lects 4-6.

TABLE 21a
MEMBERSHIP IN NOT NEGATION LECTS
BASED ON AGE OF
SIGN LANGUAGE ACQUISITION

Lects	+Before 6	- Before 6	Totals
1	25	14	39
2	29	29	58
3	5	9	14
4	4	17	21
5	1	1	2
6	1	6	7
Totals	65	76	141

TABLE 21b
A 2 BY 2 REPRESENTATION OF TABLE 21a

Lects	+Before 6	-Before 6
1-3	59 (91%)	52 (68%)
4-6	6 (9%)	24 (32%)

A x-square test of this data shows a very strong dependency relationship (to the .005 level) of ±before 6 and membership in Not Negation lects. One is more likely to find a person who learned signs before the age of six in lects 1-3 and more likely to find a person who acquired signs after the age of six in lects 4-6.

TABLE 22a
MEMBERSHIP IN NOT NEGATION LECTS BASED ON EDUCATION*

Lects	+College	-College	Totals
1	8	27	35
2	26	21	47
3	2	4	6
4	8	7	15
5	0	0	0
6	0	5	5
Totals	44	64	108

*Hearing informants are not included in this chart

TABLE 22b
A 2 BY 2 REPRESENTATION OF TABLE 22a

Lects	+College	-College
1-3	36 (82%)	52 (81%)
4-6	81 (18%)	12 (19%)

A x-square test of this data shows no dependency relationship between education and membership in Not Negation lects.

From Tables 19-22, we can state that membership in Not Negation lects is related to the variables ±deaf (lects 1-2, 3-6), ±deaf parents and ±before 6 (lects 1-3, 4-6). Deaf people from deaf parents who learn signs before the age of six are in the lects that approach pure signed English more closely. There is no relationship between education and membership in Not Negation lects. Other variables may also be related to membership in these lects.

5.2.3 Not Negation Rule.

We have already seen that verbs that may take the Negative Incorporation rule may be described by weighted cherological features. To describe the Not Negation rule, which in reality is a blocking of the Negative Incorporation rule, we need only to reverse the ± on the weights on the α, β, γ features, since the Not Negation rule follows a reverse implication from the Negative Incorporation rule. Table 23 shows the weighting necessary to describe Not Negation.

TABLE 23
WEIGHTED FEATURES ON NOT NEGATION VERBS THAT MAY TAKE NEGATIVE INCORPORATION

"good"	"know"	"want"	"like"	"have"
		α-apd	α-apd	α-apd
ßbody	ß body		ß body	ß body
	γ-out	γ-out		γ-out

If we accept the hypothesis that in the underlying structure of each sentence there is a verb "say", the underlying structure of all sentences would be Xa.

Xa.

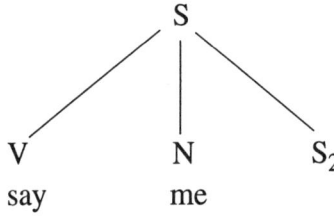

A structure like Xa would allow us an easy and reasonable solution of the problem of incorporating both the Negative Incorporation and Not Negation (really *variable bilingual* competence into the same polylectal grammar). We can mark the second S node with a feature to denote language usage, e.g., ± American Sign Language. Later the grammar can contain a rule to the following effect (Rule 2):

where S_2 is + American Sign Language, let the
Negative Incorporation rule apply';
where S_2 is −American Sign Language the
Negative Incorporation rule is blocked in the order

V
+Neg Inc
α−apd
ßbody
γ−out sig

An underlying structure such as Xa has a further advantage of allowing the grammarian to specify social variables on the speaker (modifications on the basic structure could allow for other variables to be represented). We have seen that some social variables seem to inhibit or promote operation of the rules for negation. Once we understood the relationship between these variables and language use better, we could mark the speaker with weighted features to promote or inhibit rules or language choice.

Chapter VI
Variation in Agent-Beneficiary Directionality

6.1 Outward-Inward Agent-Beneficiary Directionality.
6.1.1 Outward-Inward Agent-Beneficiary Implication.

American Sign Language has number of verbs that express the relationship between agent (actor) and beneficiary (dative) by direction of movement in three dimensional space. The verb sign begins at the agent (or at a point in his direction) and moves to the beneficiary (or a point in his direction). Although directionality may be used for all three persons, only second-person-as-agent directionality is considered in this study. The following example shows the derivational history of a typical example of second-person-as-agent directionality.

3.

$G^{\perp}$ $O_a{}^{\eta}_T$ $G_T{}^T$

YOU   GIVE   ME

"you   give   me"
(Note: the signs "you" and "me" may be deleted)

Example 3 can be seen as coming from the underlying structure represented in

3a.

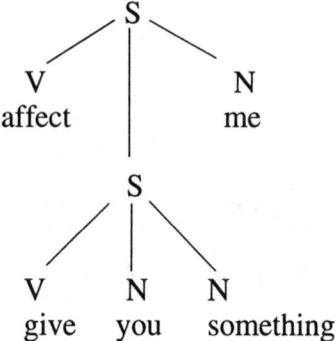

Affect is deleted and *me* is marked with +benefactive and sister adjoined to the other two noun phrases yielding

3b.

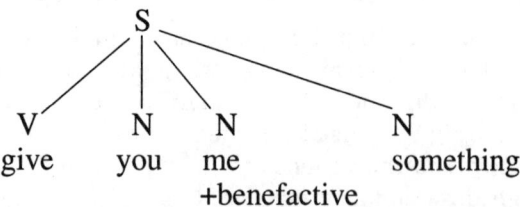

From 3b. we can assign rules that will give the correct order of elements, assign the proper direction to the verb (from agent to beneficiary), and delete all N elements that are +understood (from previous statements).

However, there is variation in signs as to which verbs can take second person directionality. This study tested nine verbs that were observed to take this directionality occasionally. These nine verbs were found to be implicationally ordered as follows:

"fingerspell" ⊃ "hate" ⊃ "hit" ⊃ "force" ⊃ "say no" ⊃ "ask (question)" ⊃ "tell" ⊃ "give" ⊃ "show".

This implication produces the ten possible lects listed in Table 24. For 141 persons at nine slots a person, there is a total of 1,296 slots. There were 131 exceptions (listed in the Appen-

TABLE 24
IMPLICATIONAL LECTS FOR OUTWARD-INWARD AGENT-BENEFICIARY DIRECTIONALITY

Lects	$5_\lor^\alpha$ "fingerspell"	$88\dot{\square}_\perp$ "hate"	$G_{\land o} A\dot{L}^{\dot x}_\perp$ "hit"	$\bar{\jmath} C_\lor^\perp$ "force"	$3_\perp^{\ddot{\#}}$ "say no"	$G_{\#\perp}^{\square}$ "ask"	$\cup G_<^\perp$ "tell"	$O_\alpha^\perp$ "give"	$B^! G_<^\perp$ "show"
1	+	+	+	+	+	+	+	+	+
2	–	+	+	+	+	+	+	+	+
3	–	–	+	+	+	+	+	+	+
4	–	–	–	+	+	+	+	+	+
5	–	–	–	–	+	+	+	+	+
6	–	–	–	–	–	+	+	+	+
7	–	–	–	–	–	–	+	+	+
8	–	–	–	–	–	–	–	+	+
9	–	–	–	–	–	–	–	–	+
10	–	–	–	–	–	–	–	–	–

dix) in the responses, yielding a 10.1% rate of exception or a 89.9% rate of acceptability, a strongly valid implication.

The incorporation of the information supplied by the implication in the grammar of American Sign Language is discussed after the following section on the relation of Outward-Inward Agent-Beneficiary lects with social class.

6.1.2 Relation of Outward-Inward Agent-Beneficiary Lects with Social Variables.

Table 25 shows the distribution in Outward-Inward Agent-Beneficiary lects 1-10 according to grouping based on the four social variables of the study.

TABLE 25
MEMBERSHIP IN OUTWARD-INWARD AGENT-BENEFICIARY LECTS

Groups Deaf	+D	+D	+D	+D	+D	+D	−D	−D	Total
Deaf Parents	+DP	+DP	−DP	−DP	−DP	−DP	+DP	−DP	
Before 6	+B6	+B6	+B6	+B6	−B6	−B6	+B6	−B6	
College	+C	−C	+C	−C	+C	−C	+C	+C	
Lects									
1	2	1	3	1	1	1	0	1	10
2	5	1	4	9	5	8	3	0	35
3	0	3	1	1	4	1	2	1	13
4	1	4	2	1	3	1	0	0	12
5	2	0	2	1	2	7	1	0	15
6	2	1	0	0	0	4	0	3	10
7	1	1	0	3	2	5	1	4	17
8	0	1	0	0	0	1	0	1	3
9	0	0	0	1	1	0	0	6	8
10	1	1	0	0	0	6	2	8	18
Totals	14	13	12	17	18	34	9	24	141

It is possible to look at membership in the lects with relationship to each of the social variables. Tables 26-29 show these relationships.

TABLE 26a
MEMBERSHIP IN OUTWARD-INWARD AGENT-BENEFICIARY LECTS BY DEAFNESS

Lects	+Deaf	-Deaf	Total
1	9	1	10
2	32	3	35
3	10	3	13
4	12	0	12
5	14	1	15
6	7	3	10
7	12	5	17
8	2	1	3
9	2	6	8
10	8	10	18
Totals	108	33	141

Lects 1-5 comprise the half of the implicational scale that approaches American Sign Language more closely, that is the half of the implicational scale that uses Outward-Inward Agent-Beneficiary Directionality in the most environments. Setting up a 2 by 2 chart we can test the significance of the variable ± deaf and membership in Outward-Inward Agent-Beneficiary lects.

TABLE 26b
A 2 BY 2 REPRESENTATION OF TABLE 26a

Lects	+Deaf	-Deaf
1-5	77 (71%)	8 (24%)
6-10	31 (29%)	25 (76%)

A x-square test of this data shows a very strong dependency relationship (at the .005 level) of ±deaf and membership in the lects. One is more likely to find a deaf person in lects 1-5 (closer to ASL) and more likely to find a hearing person in lects 6-10 (further from ASL).

TABLE 27a
MEMBERSHIP IN OUTWARD-INWARD AGENT-BENEFICIARY LECTS BY PARENTAGE

Lects	+Deaf Parents	-Deaf Parents	Total
1	3	7	10
2	9	26	35
3	5	8	13
4	5	7	12
5	3	12	15
6	3	7	10
7	3	14	17
8	1	2	3
9	0	8	8
10	4	14	18
Totals	36	105	141

TABLE 27b
A 2 BY 2 REPRESENTATION OF TABLE 27a

Lects	+Deaf Parents	-Deaf Parents
1-5	25 (69%)	60 (57%)
6-10	11 (31%)	45 (43%)

A x-square test of this data shows no dependency relationship of ±deaf parents and membership in these lects.

TABLE 28a
MEMBERSHIP IN OUTWARD-INWARD AGENT-BENEFICIARY LECTS BY AGE OF SIGN LANGUAGE ACQUISITION

Lects	+Before 6	-Before 6	Total
1	7	3	10
2	22	13	35
3	7	6	13
4	8	4	12
5	6	9	15
6	3	7	10
7	6	11	17
8	1	2	3
9	1	7	8
10	4	14	18
Totals	65	76	141

TABLE 28b
A 2 BY 2 REPRESENTATION OF TABLE 28a

Lects	+Before 6	-Before 6
1-5	50 (77%)	35 (46%)
6-10	15 (23%)	41 (54%)

A x-square test of the data shows a strong relationship of the variable ±before six and membership in these lects. One is more likely to find a person who learned signs before 6 in lects 1-5 (closer to ASL) and more likely to find a person who learned signs after 6 in lects 6-10 (further from ASL).

TABLE 29a
MEMBERSHIP IN OUTWARD-INWARD AGENT-BENEFICIARY LECTS BY EDUCATION*

Lects	+College	-College	Total
1	6	3	9
2	14	18	32
3	5	5	10
4	6	6	12
5	6	8	14
6	2	5	7
7	3	9	12
8	0	2	2
9	1	1	2
10	1	7	8
Totals	44	64	108

*Hearing Informants are not included in this chart.

TABLE 29b
A 2 BY 2 REPRESENTATION OF TABLE 29a

Lects	+College	-College
1-5	37 (84%)	32 (50%)
6-10	7 (16%)	32 (50%)

A x-square test of this data shows a very strong dependency relationship (at the .005 level) of ±college and membership in these lects. One is more likely to find a deaf person who has attended some college in lects 1-5 (closer to ASL) and more likely to find a deaf person who has not attended any college in lects 6-10 (further from ASL).

Tables 26-29 have demonstrated that there are very strong dependency relationships between the variables ±deaf, ±before 6 and ±college and membership in Outward-Inward Agent-Beneficiary lects. As intuitively expected, deaf persons who learned signs before the age of six are more likely to be in lects that approach ASL more closely. However, there is no dependency relationship between ±deaf parents and relationship in these lects.

TABLE 30a
FEATURES ON OUTWARD-INWARD AGENT-BENEFICIARY VERBS

Feature*	"finger spell"	"hate"	"hit"	"force"	"say no"	"ask"	"tell"	"give"	"show"
present	–pre	–pre	–pre	–pre	–pre	–pre	–pre	+pre	+pre
say	–say	–say	–say	–say	+say	+say	+say	–say	–say
harm	–harm	+harm	+harm	+harm	–harm	–harm	–harm	–harm	–harm
movement	+move	+move	–move	–move	+move	+move	–move	–move	–move
fore	+fore	+fore	–fore	+fore	–fore	+fore	+fore	–fore	+fore

*Semantic and phonological features are necessary to describe this variation.

TABLE 30b
WEIGHTED FEATURES ON OUTWARD-INWARD AGENT-BENEFICIARY VERBS

"finger spell"	"hate"	"hit"	"force"	"say no"	"ask"	"tell"	"give"	"show"
				β say	β say	β say	α pre	α pre
	γ harm	γ harm	γ harm					
		δ-move	δ-move			δ-move	δ-move	δ-move
ε fore	ε fore		ε fore		ε fore	ε fore		ε fore

6.1.3 Outward-Inward Agent-Beneficiary Rule.

It is possible to incorporate the information supplied by the Outward-Inward Agent-Beneficiary implication into the grammar. Those features which serve to distinguish the nine Outward-Inward Agent-Beneficiary verbs are shown in Table 30a. Inspection of Table 30a shows that these features form a weighted context of features. In Table 30b, the weightings are shown and letters α to ε are assigned in order: the α feature most strongly influences operation of the rule; the ε feature the least.

The rule of Outward-Inward Agent-Beneficiary Directionality can now be written. Later rules will allow for deletion of all N +understood.

[N   V   N   ]
s α pre   +benefactive   s
       ß say
       γ harm
       δ-move
       ε fore

1   2   3   4   5 $\Rightarrow$

1   2   3   4   5
           + in sig

6.2 Outward-Only Agent-Beneficiary Directionality.

6.2.1 Outward-Only Agent-Beneficiary Implication.

As one approaches the English part of the continuum, inward directionality for the second person on Agent-Beneficiary verbs is used less. The most "pure" English signing has outward only directionality for all agent-beneficiary relationships. The derivational history of a typical example of Outward-Only Agent-Beneficiary Directionality follows.

Note that the underlying structures of both Outward-Inward Agent-Beneficiary Directionality and Outward-Only Agent-Beneficiary Directionality are the same; surface structure representations differ radically, however.

4.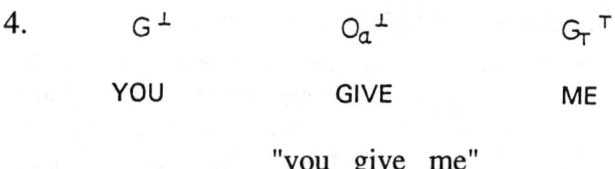

"you give me"

Example 4 has the same underlying structure as example 3.

4a. (3a.)

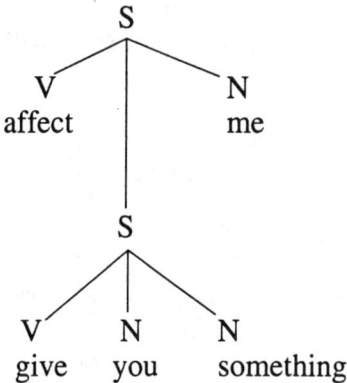

Affect is deleted and *me* is marked with +benefactive and sister adjoined to the other two noun phrases.

4f. (3f.)

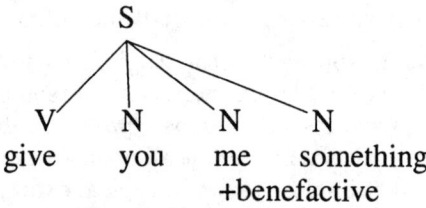

At this point in the derivation, if Outward-Only Directionality is used, rules that assign direction and rules that allow deletion of +understood N's are blocked. The verb is assigned an outward sig and English word order, cases and tenses are assigned.

There is variation in signs as to which verbs can take outward-only second person directionality. The nine verbs tested in this study were found to be implicationally ordered, however, the implication is not the reverse of the implication for Outward-Inward Agent-Beneficiary Directionality. The verbs are ordered as follows: "ask" ⊃ "give" ⊃ "say no" ⊃ "tell" ⊃ "force" ⊃ "hit" ⊃ "show" ⊃ "hate" ⊃ "fingerspell".

As was mentioned in Chapter 5, we would normally expect this implication to be the mirror image of the Outward-Inward Agent Beneficiary implication. However, it is not. The reason for this is still unclear. As mentioned before in Chapter 5, perhaps it is because we are dealing with variable bilingual competence. Or perhaps this construction is not salient in Signed English and thus yields a freak implicational phenomenon. It should be noted here that there is no dependency relationship between any of the four social variables chosen for this study and membership in Outward-Only Agent-Beneficiary lects. But, the very fact that this is an implication indicates there is regularity in the variation of the construction.

Whatever the reason for the non-occurrence of the mirror image implication may be, the non-occurrence is interesting and awaits further investigation. The implication generates ten possible lects. These lects are shown in Table 31.

TABLE 31

IMPLICATIONAL LECTS FOR OUTWARD-ONLY
AGENT-BENEFICIARY LECTS

Lects	"ask"	"give"	"say no"	"tell"	"force"	"hit"	"show"	"hate"	"fingerspell"
1	+	+	+	+	+	+	+	+	+
2	−	+	+	+	+	+	+	+	+
3	−	−	+	+	+	+	+	+	+
4	−	−	−	+	+	+	+	+	+
5	−	−	−	−	+	+	+	+	+
6	−	−	−	−	−	+	+	+	+
7	−	−	−	−	−	−	+	+	+
8	−	−	−	−	−	−	−	+	+
9	−	−	−	−	−	−	−	−	+
10	−	−	−	−	−	−	−	−	−

With 141 informants completing questionnaires about nine verbs, the total responses numbered 1,296. Of these 141 or 10.9% (listed in the Appendix) did not fit into the implicational scale, giving a 89.1% rate of following the implication. Thus this implication is valid.

The information supplied by the implication will be incorporated into the grammar after the following discussion on the relation of Outward Only Agent-Beneficiary lects with social variables

6.2.2 Relation of Outward-Only Agent-Beneficiary Lects with Social Variables.

Table 32 shows the distribution in Outward-Only Agent-Beneficiary lects 1-10 according to grouping based on the four social variables of the study.

TABLE 32
MEMBERSHIP IN OUTWARD-ONLY AGENT-BENEFICIARY LECTS

Groups Deaf Deaf Parents Before 6 College	+D +DP +B6 +C	+D +DP +B6 −C	+D −DP +B6 +C	+D −DP +B6 −C	+D −DP −B6 +C	+D −DP −B6 −C	−D +DP +B6 +C	−D −DP −B6 +C	Total
Lects									
1	2	3	4	6	2	7	3	2	29
2	0	1	1	4	2	5	2	7	22
3	3	3	2	4	3	10	0	3	28
4	4	2	2	3	7	3	2	2	25
5	2	2	0	0	1	1	0	4	10
6	1	1	0	0	0	2	0	1	5
7	0	0	0	0	1	2	1	0	4
8	0	0	0	0	1	0	0	3	4
9	2	1	3	0	1	2	1	2	12
10	0	0	0	0	0	2	0	0	2
Totals	14	13	12	17	18	34	9	24	141

It is also possible to look at membership in lects with relationship to each of the social variables. Tables 33-36 show the relationships.

TABLE 33a
MEMBERSHIP IN OUTWARD-ONLY AGENT-BENEFICIARY LECTS BY DEAFNESS

Lects	+Deaf	-Deaf	Total
1	24	5	29
2	13	9	22
3	25	3	28
4	21	4	25
5	6	4	10
6	4	1	5
7	3	1	4
8	1	3	4
9	9	3	12
10	2	0	2
Totals	108	33	141

Lects 1-5 comprise the half of the implicational scale that approaches Signed English more closely, that is, the half of the implicational scale that accepts Outward-Only Agent-Beneficiary Directionality in the most environments. Setting up a 2 by 2 chart, we can test the significance of the variable +deaf and membership in Outward-Only Agent-Beneficiary lects.

TABLE 33b
A 2 BY 2 REPRESENTATION OF TABLE 33a

Lects	+Deaf	-Deaf
1-5	89 (82%)	25 (76%)
6-10	19 (18%)	8 (24%)

A x-square test of this data shows no dependency relationship between the variable ±deaf and membership in these lects.

TABLE 34a
MEMBERSHIP IN OUTWARD-ONLY AGENT-BENEFICIARY LECTS BY PARENTAGE

Lects	+Deaf Parents	–Deaf Parents	Total
1	8	21	29
2	3	19	22
3	6	22	28
4	8	17	25
5	4	6	10
6	2	3	5
7	1	3	4
8	0	4	4
9	4	8	12
10	0	2	2
Totals	36	105	141

TABLE 34b
A 2 BY 2 REPRESENTATION OF TABLE 34a

Lects	+Deaf Parents	-Deaf Parents
1-5	29 (81%)	85 (81%)
6-10	7 (19%)	20 (19%)

A x-square test of this data show no dependency relationship of the variable ±deaf parents and membership in these lects.

TABLE 35a
MEMBERSHIP IN OUTWARD-ONLY AGENT-BENEFICIARY LECTS BY AGE OF SIGN LANGUAGE ACQUISITION

Lects	+Before 6	–Before 6	Total
1	18	11	29
2	8	14	22
3	12	16	28
4	13	12	25
5	4	6	10
6	2	3	5
7	1	3	4
8	0	4	4
9	7	5	12
10	0	2	2
Totals	65	76	141

TABLE 35b
A 2 BY 2 REPRESENTATION OF TABLE 35a

Lects	+Before 6	-Before 6
1-5	55 (85%)	59 (78%)
6-10	10 (15%)	17 (22%)

A x-square test of this data shows no dependency relationship of the variable +before 6 and membership in these lects.

TABLE 36a
MEMBERSHIP IN OUTWARD-ONLY AGENT-BENEFICIARY LECTS BY EDUCATION*

Lects	+College	-College	Total
1	8	16	24
2	3	10	13
3	8	17	25
4	13	8	21
5	3	3	6
6	1	3	4
7	1	2	3
8	1	0	1
9	6	3	9
10	0	2	2
Totals	44	64	108

*Hearing informants are not included in Table 36a.

TABLE 36b
A 2 BY 2 REPRESENTATION OF TABLE 36a

Lects	+College	-College
1-5	35 (80%)	54 (84%)
6-10	9 (20%)	10 (16%)

A x-square test of this data shows no dependency relationship of the variable ±college and membership in these lects. Tables 33-36 have shown no dependency relationships of any of the social variables and membership in Outward-Only Agent-Beneficiary lects. This seems strange. Perhaps Outward-Only Agent-Beneficiary Directionality is not a salient rule in Signed English. It may be true that membership in these lects is related to some other social variable.

TABLE 37a
FEATURES ON OUTWARD-ONLY AGENT-BENEFICIARY VERBS

Feature*	"ask"	"give"	"say no"	"tell"	"force"	"hit"	"show"	"hate"	"finger spell"
close	+clo	–clo	+clo	+clo	–clo	+clo	+clo	–clo	–clo
bent	+bent	–bent	–bent	–bent	+bent	–bent	–bent	–bent	–bent
flexible	–flex	–flex	–flex	–flex	+flex	+flex	+flex	–flex	–flex
mid	–mid	–mid	–mid	–mid	+mid	–mid	–mid	–mid	+mid
fore	+fore	–fore	–fore	+fore	+fore	–fore	+fore	+fore	+fore

*Only phonological features are necessary to describe this variation.

TABLE 37b
WEIGHTED FEATURES ON OUTWARD-ONLY AGENT-BENEFICIARY VERBS*

"ask"	"say no"	"tell"	"force"	"hit"	"show"	"hate"	"finger-spell"
α-bent	α-bent	α-bent	α-close	α-bent	α-bent	α-close	α-close
						α-bent	α-bent
				β flex	β flex		
			γ mid				γ mid
δ fore		δ fore	δ fore		δ fore	δ fore	δ fore

* "give" does not fit the implication with this analysis; "give" may be a lexical exception.

6.2.3 Outward-Only Agent-Beneficiary Rule.

It is possible to incorporate the information supplied by the Outward-Only Agent-Beneficiary implication into the grammar. Those features which serve to distinguish the nine Outward-Only Agent-Beneficiary verbs are shown in Table 37a. Inspection of Table 37a shows that these features form a weighted context of features. In Table 37b, the weightings are shown and letters α - δ are assigned in order: the α features most strongly influence operation of the rule: the δ feature the least.

The rule for Outward-Only Agent-Beneficiary Directionality can now be written.
This rule will block the Outward-Inward Agent-Beneficiary rule and deletion rules for all N
+understood

For now, "give" will have to be listed as a lexical exception.

[N   V   N   ]
s   a-close +benefactives
                α-bent
                β flex
                γ mid
                δ fore
1   2   3   4   5 $\Rightarrow$
1   2   3   4   5
              +out sig

Chapter VII
Variation in Verb Reduplication

7.1 Verb Reduplication Implication.

The third and final type of variation examined in this study is reduplication of verbs. Reduplication is a productive grammatical process in numerous languages, e.g., Chinese. As with many languages that have surface verb reduplication, reduplication in American Sign Language verbs may come from several underlying structures (Fischer, MS), but it seems that the most basic underlying structure is one that contains a semantic verb *continue*. The derivational history of an example of Verb Reduplication follows:

5.

$L^{\text{II}}L_{\perp}^{\text{Q}}$ $L^{\text{II}}L_{\perp}^{\text{Q}}$ $G_T^{\ T}$
RUN   RUN   ME

"I   am (was)   running"

The underlying structure for this sentence is posited in 5a on the following page.

5a

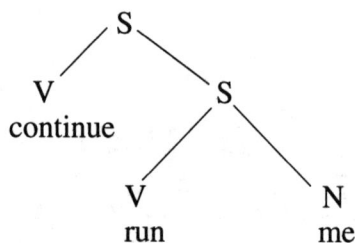

By predicate lowering 5b is obtained.

5b.

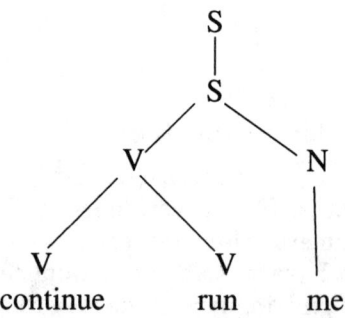

Tree pruning allows us to delete the highest S node, producing 5c.

5c.

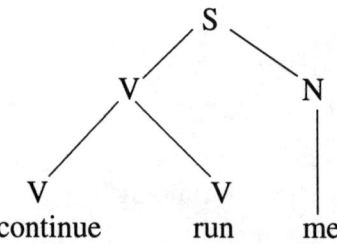

A grammar closer to Signed English will change the word order and give a surface symbolization to each of these lexical units. A grammar closer to American Sign Language, however, will rewrite the verb *continue* as *run* and then give a final surface symbolization to the forms. Rewriting the verb continue would yield the tree in 5d.

5d.

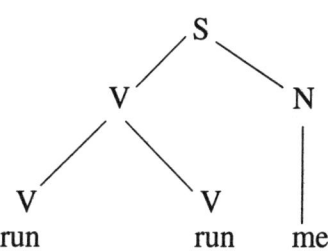

There seems to be a large number of verbs that can be reduplicated, however, not everyone who signs reduplicates the same verbs. This study tested reduplication in nine verbs: "read", "want", "drive", "memorize", "study", "see", "run", "know", "meet". Responses to the questionnaire show an implicational ordering of: "meet" ⊃ "memorize" ⊃ "see" ⊃ "want" ⊃ "study" ⊃ "read" ⊃ "know" ⊃ "run" ⊃ "drive".

Based on this implicational ordering there are ten possible lects. Table 38 shows these lects.

With nine verbs and 141 informants, there is a total of 1,269 possible slots. There were 119 exceptions (listed in the Appendix), yielding a 9.4% rate for exceptions or a 90.6% rate of acceptability, which indicates that the implication is strongly valid.

The information supplied by the implication must be incorporated into the grammar. Methodology for doing this will be discussed after the following discussion of the relation of these lects with social variables

TABLE 38
IMPLICATIONAL LECTS FOR VERB REDUPLICATION

Lects	$G_\wedge{}^!G_\wedge{}^\times$ "meet"	$\cap 5_T{}_\perp \#[A]$ "memorize"	$\sqcup V_T{}_\perp$ "see"	$C_\alpha C_\alpha{}^\top$ "want"	$B_\alpha\ 5_v{}^\alpha$ "study"	$B_T\ V_D{}^\vee$ "read"	$\cap B_T{}^\times$ "know"	$L^\pi L^\alpha_\perp$ "run"	$AA^{N\sim}$ "drive"
1	+	+	+	+	+	+	+	+	+
2	–	+	+	+	+	+	+	+	+
3	–	–	+	+	+	+	+	+	+
4	–	–	–	+	+	+	+	+	+
5	–	–	–	+	+	+	+	+	+
6	–	–	–	–	+	+	+	+	+
7	–	–	–	–	–	+	+	+	+
8	–	–	–	–	–	–	+	+	+
9	–	–	–	–	–	–	–	–	+
10	–	–	–	–	–	–	–	–	–

TABLE 39
MEMBERSHIP IN VERB REDUPLICATION LECTS

Groups:
- Deaf
- Deaf Parents
- Before six
- College

Lects	+D +DP +B6 +C	+D +DP +B6 -C	+D -DP +B6 +C	+D -DP +B6 -C	+D -DP -B6 +C	+D -DP -B6 -C	-D +DP +B6 +C	-D -DP -B6 +C	Totals
1	3	9	6	5	11	9	1	2	46
2	7	2	3	3	4	4	4	3	30
3	2	1	1	2	1	5	1	0	13
4	0	0	0	2	1	7	0	1	11
5	2	1	2	3	1	3	2	6	20
6	0	0	0	1	0	2	0	1	4
7	0	0	0	1	0	0	0	2	3
8	0	0	0	0	0	0	0	3	3
9	0	0	0	0	0	0	0	2	2
10	0	0	0	0	0	4	1	4	9
Totals	14	13	12	17	18	34	9	24	141

7.2 Relation of Verb Reduplication Lects with Social Variables.

Table 39 shows membership in each of the verb reduplication lects based on the four social variables chosen for this study.

It is possible to look at membership in the lects with relationship to each of the social variables. Tables 40-43 show the relationships.

TABLE 40a
MEMBERSHIP IN VERB REDUPLICATION LECTS BASED ON DEAFNESS

Lects	+Deaf	–Deaf	Totals
1	43	3	46
2	23	7	30
3	12	1	13
4	10	1	11
5	12	8	20
6	3	1	4
7	1	2	3
8	0	3	3
9	0	2	2
10	0	9	9
Totals	108	33	141

Lects 1-5 comprise the half of the implicational scale that approaches "pure" American Sign Language more closely, that is, the half of the implicational scale that uses American Sign Language Verb Reduplication in the most environments. Setting up a 2 by 2 chart, we can test significance of the variable ±deaf and membership in Verb Reduplication lects.

TABLE 40b
A 2 BY 2 REPRESENTATION OF TABLE 40a

Lects	+Deaf	-Deaf
1-5	100 (93%)	20 (61%)
6-10	8 (7%)	13 (39%)

A x-square test of this data shows a very strong dependence relationship (to the .005 level) of ±deaf and membership in Verb Reduplication lects. One is more likely to find a deaf person in lects 1-5 (closer to ASL) and more likely to find a hearing person in lects 6-10 (further from ASL).

TABLE 41a
MEMBERSHIP IN VERB REDUPLICATION LECTS BASED ON PARENTAGE

Lects	+Deaf Parents	–Deaf Parents	Totals
1	13	33	46
2	13	17	30
3	4	9	13
4	0	11	11
5	5	15	20
6	0	4	4
7	0	3	3
8	0	3	3
9	0	2	2
10	1	8	9
Totals	36	105	141

TABLE 41b
A 2 BY 2 REPRESENTATION OF TABLE 41a

Lects	+Deaf Parents	-Deaf Parents
1-5	35 (97%)	85 (81%)
6-10	1 (3%)	20 (19%)

A x-square test of this data shows a dependency relationship (at the .05 level) of ±deaf parents and membership in Verb Reduplication lects. One is more likely to find a person with deaf parents in lects 1-5 (closer to ASL) and more likely to find a person with hearing parents in lects 6-10 (further from ASL).

TABLE 42a
MEMBERSHIP IN VERB REDUPLICATION LECTS BASED ON AGE OF SIGN LANGUAGE ACQUISITION

Lects	+Before 6	-Before 6	Totals
1	33	13	46
2	19	11	30
3	7	6	13
4	2	9	11
5	12	8	20
6	1	3	4
7	1	2	3
8	0	3	3
9	0	2	2
10	1	8	9
Totals	76	65	141

TABLE 42b
A 2 BY 2 REPRESENTATION OF TABLE 42a

Lects	+Before 6	-Before 6
1-5	73 (96%)	47 (72%)
6-10	3 (4%)	18 (28%)

A x-square test of this data shows a very strong dependency relationship (at the .005 level) of ±before 6 and membership in Verb Reduplication lects. One is more likely to find a person who learned signs before the age of six in lects 1-5 (closer to ASL) and more likely to find a person who learned signs after the age of six in lects 6-10 (further from ASL).

TABLE 43a
MEMBERSHIP IN VERB REDUPLICATION LECTS BASED ON EDUCATION*

Lects	+College	-College	Totals
1	20	23	43
2	14	9	23
3	4	8	12
4	1	9	10
5	5	7	12
6	0	3	3
7	0	1	1
8	0	0	0
9	0	0	0
10	0	4	4
Totals	44	64	108

*Hearing informants are not included in this chart.

TABLE 43b
A 2 BY 2 REPRESENTATION OF TABLE 43a

Lects	+College	-College
1-5	44 (100%)	56 (88%)
6-10	0 (0%)	8 (12%)

A x-square test of this data shows a strong dependency relationship (at the .04 level) between education (of deaf informants) and membership in Verb Reduplication lects.

From Tables 40-43, we can state that membership in Verb Reduplication lects is related to all four of the social variables used in this study. As one would intuitively expect, informants who are deaf, from deaf parents and who learned signs before the age of six are in the lects that approach American Sign Language more closely.

TABLE 44a
FEATURES ON REDUPLICATED VERBS

Feature*	"meet"	"memorize"	"see"	"want"	"study"	"read"	"know"	"run"	"drive"
spread	−spr	+spr	+spr	+spr	+spr	+spr	−spr	−spr	−spr
high	−high	+high	+high	−high	−high	−high	+high	−high	−high
closing mov'mt	−clm	+clm	−clm	+clm	−clm	−clm	−clm	−clm	−clm
closed	+clo	+clo	+clo	−clo	−clo	+clo	−clo	+clo	+clo
bent	−bent	+bent	−bent	+bent	−bent	−bent	−bent	+bent	−bent

7.3 Verb Reduplication Rule.

It is possible to write a rule that will incorporate the information supplied by the implication in the grammar. Table 44a lists the features necessary to describe the verbs which reduplicate.

We can now weight these features, assigning α to the heaviest (or earliest) environment in which the rule applies. Table 44b shows the verbs with their proper weighting.

TABLE 44b
WEIGHTED FEATURES ON REDUPLICATED VERBS

"memorize"	"see"	"want"	"study"	"read"	"know"	"run"	"drive"
		β-high	β-high	β-high	α-spr	α-spr	α-spr
	γ-clm		γ-clm	γ-clm	β-high	β-high	β-high
δ clo	δ clo			δ clo	γ-clm	γ-clm	γ-clm
ε-bent	ε-bent		ε-bent	ε-bent	ε-bent	δ clo	δ clo
							ε-bent

There is one exception, however, 'meet'. According to the weighting, 'meet' should be at the other end of the implication. There are four possible reasons for this exception:
(1) The hierarchy of features is wrong.
(2) 'meet' differs in only one feature from the verb meaning 'to have intercourse with' and in fast signing there might be misunderstanding.
(3) 'meet' has a semantic feature in American Sign Language which overrides phonological constraints.
(4) 'meet' is a lexical exception.

The most reasonable answers to the problem seem to be 3 or 4. The weighting of features given explains 8/9ths of the data. People accustomed to signing also probably have no trouble distinguishing between 'meet' and 'to have intercourse with', even though there is only a small distinction. Until further data is obtained 'meet' will have to be listed as a lexical exception.

The rule for Verb Reduplication which changed tree 5c to 5d can now be formulated.

Rule 5 [[Continue +Verb Reduplication]   N   ]
     S   V α-spr   V   S
     +ASL β-high
                      γ-clm
                      δ clo
                      ϵ-bent

1   2   3   4   5   6   7=
1   2   4   4   5   6   7

Chapter VIII
Research Implications

8.1 Results of the Study.
8.1.1 The Implications.

This study tested five linguistic variables to determine if they formed implicational patterns. These variables were Negative Incorporation, Not Negation, Outward-Inward Agent-Beneficiary Directionality, Outward-Only Agent-Beneficiary Directionality, and Verb Reduplication. All of these variables were 89%-97% implicationally scalable indicating that these are strongly valid implications.

8.1.2 Relation of the Implications with Social Variables.

For the purpose of relating membership in the implicational lects with the four social variables, each of the implications were split in half before x-square tests were applied to the data.

8.1.2.1 Negative Incorporation Lects.

Membership in Negative Incorporation lects was found to relate with the variable ±deaf. That is, one is more likely to find that a deaf person's signs pattern in lects that use Negative Incorporation in the most environments and more likely to find that a hearing person's signs pattern in lects that use Negative Incorporation in fewer environments.

8.1.2.2 Not Negation Lects.

Membership in Not Negation lects was found to relate with the variables ±deaf, ±deaf parents, and ±before 6. That is, one is more likely to find that the signs of a deaf person, a person with deaf parents, and a person who learned signs before the age of six pattern in lects that use Not Negation in the most environments. Likewise, one is more likely to find that the signs of a hearing person, a person with hearing parents, and a person who learned signs after the age of six pattern in lects that use Not Negation in fewer environments.

8.1.2.3 Outward-Inward Agent-Beneficiary Lects.

Membership in these lects was found to relate with the variables ±deaf, ±deaf parents, and ±college. That is, one is more likely to find that the signs of a deaf person, a person with deaf parents, and a deaf person who has attended some college pattern in lects that use Outward-Inward Agent-Beneficiary Directionality in the most environments. Likewise, one is more likely to find that the signs of a hearing person, a person with hearing parents, and a deaf person who has not attended any college pattern in lects that use Outward-Inward Agent-Beneficiary Directionality in fewer environments.

8.1.2.4 Outward-Only Agent-Beneficiary Lects.

Membership in these lects was not found to relate with any of the social variables.

8.1.2.5 Verb Reduplication Lects.

Membership in Verb Reduplication lects was found to relate with all four variables. One is more likely to find that the signs of a deaf person, a person with deaf parents, a person who learned signs before the age of six, and a person who has attended some college pattern in lects that use Verb Reduplication in the most environments. Likewise, one is more likely to find that the signs of a hearing person, a person with hearing parents, a person who learned signs after the age of six, and person who has not attended any college pattern in lects that use Verb Reduplication in fewer environments.

8.1.3 Cherological Features.

As was mentioned in Chapter 1, the cherological features that have been posited for tabs (Battison and Woodward, 1972) and dezes (Battison, Friedman, and Zambrano, 1972) were considered highly speculative. However, the features are adequate to write weighted rules to describe almost all the information supplied by each of the implications. There were two exceptions: "give" in Outward-Only Agent-Beneficiary Lects and "meet" in Verb Reduplication. Further research in sign language cherology may be able to explain these exceptions in terms of cherological features or to show that they truly are lexical exceptions.

8.2 Implications of the Study.

8.2.1 Variation Theory.

One of the objectives of this study was to test variation theory on a visual language -- a phenomenon which most linguists have not studied. Implicational analysis, statistical relations of linguistic variables with social variables, and weighted rules all are adequate to describe and explain the complex but regular variation on the deaf diglossic continuum.

8.2.1.1 Implicational Analysis.

As mentioned earlier in this chapter, all of the five linguistic variables used in this study were found to be 89% - 97% scalable -- strongly valid implications.

However, an interested situation arose. As stated in Chapter 5 and Chapter 6, we expected the Not Negation implication to be the mirror image of the Negative-Incorporation implication and we expected the Outward-Only Agent-Beneficiary implication to be the mirror image of the Outward-Inward Agent-Beneficiary implication. Not Negation acted as was expected; OutwardOnly Agent-Beneficiary Directionality did not.

There seem to be two possible reasons why Outward-Only Agent-Beneficiary Directionality patterns unexpectedly: (1) the Outward-Only Agent-Beneficiary Implication is a freak implication (See Chapter 6), (2) the Outward-Only Agent-Beneficiary implication is strange because we are dealing with bilingual, not monolingual, inherent variability. If (2) is true, then this study has shown that the non-occurrence of an expected mirror image implication is a sign that inherent variability is occurring in two separate languages. This is important, since (as was discussed in Chapter 6) present guidelines for determining the difference between one language and two are vague at best. Again it is also important to note that this non-occurrence of an expected mirror image implication has not been encountered or discussed in linguistic literature before now. It is truly unique.

8.2.1.2 Relation of Linguistic Variation with Social Variation.

Numerous recent sociolinguistic studies, e.g., Fasold 1972, have shown linguistic variation often to be related with social variation. It is interesting in this study that not all the four social variables relate with all of the linguistic variation. The most important social variable for signing seems to be deafness, which relates with four of the lectal implications. The second most important social variable seems to be age of sign language acquisition which relates with three of the lectal implications. Parentage and education relate with two of the lectal implications.

Again the Outward-Only Agent-Beneficiary implication appears to be strange, since it is the only implication that does not relate with any of the social variables.

These complex interrelationships between linguistic and social variation are interesting not only for the linguist but also for the sociologist and the educator. The relationships mark a social group with structured language varieties. The deaf should be treated as such a group.

8.2.2 American Sign Language.

This study has demonstrated that the complex variation that exists along the deaf diglossic continuum is regular and is describable within the framework of current variation theory. Grammatical variation in American Sign Language and Signed English clearly follows implicational patterns and is describable through weighted cherological and semantic features. It should be noted gain that these cherological features are unique and autonomous and have no relationship to English phonology. Different features or different ± markings on the features are necessary to describe the variation in American Sign Language as opposed to the variation in Signed English.

The implication of the above paragraph is that American Sign Language is without doubt a language with its own semantax and cherology. Even Signed English grammatical variation is conditioned by cherological features of American Sign Language not English phonology.

The information supplied by the implications can be of great help to those involved in teaching Signed English and/or American Sign Language as a second language. The implicational scales can be used as a basis for planning what variety of signs to teach and what progression to teach.

Since these implicational scales have developed naturally, it would seem only logical to follow the natural historical developments, i.e., the implications in teaching these languages. Finally, these scales should also serve as useful tools for diagnosing what kind of sign language competence the student has, since a person's membership in the lects indicates his distances from American Sign Language and from Signed English.

8.3 Future Research.

It is obvious that this study is only a small beginning toward describing signs polylectally in a dynamic framework. Much more research needs to be done.

8.3.1 Other Locations and Informants.

These five implications need to be tested in other areas of the United States, especially the South, and among other ethnic groups, especially Southern Blacks (Woodward and Erting, 1973, and Donnels, 1973).

Most researchers dealing with American Sign Language believe that there is only one American Sign Language and that variations that are found are dialectal (sic). If there is only one American Sign Language, then these implications should be valid (with *very* minor changes) for the whole U. S. If the implications are radically different, this would be strong evidence that what has been termed American Sign Language is really more than one language.

8.3.2 Other Variables.

There are numerous other grammatical variables that could be tested for implicational patterning: (1) noun reduplication, (2) variation in noun-adjective word order, and (3) copula presence, variation, and absence, to name a few. Not only grammatical but also lexical and cherological variables might be tested. Undoubtedly some, if not most, lexical and cherological variation is implicational, since this variation has historical bases and implications describe historical changes.

Cherological implications should be extremely useful in determining a person's distances from American Sign Language and from Signed English on the deaf diglossic continuum. Quite possibly investigations into cherological feature implications will also yield information that could lead to the development of marking theory and natural cherology for sign languages. Three sample hypotheses on marking in American Sign Language are: (1) if a sign language has +crossed (marked) it will also have −crossed (unmarked), e.g., an R dez implies H and/or V dezes; (2) if a sign language has +bent (marked) it will also have -bent (unmarked), e.g., an X dez implies an G dez; (3) if a sign language has +extreme (marked), it will also have −extreme (unmarked), e.g., a top of the head tab implies a forehead tab.

If the all too meager evidence from the comparative study of sign languages, child sign language development, and historical change in sign languages (as well as lectal variations) can suggest implications like the above for cherological markedness and naturalness, imagine what full scale research of the world's sign languages could accomplish for the development of linguistic theory as well as for the development of respect of sign languages as valuable and highly interesting languages.

8.4. Final Remarks.

It is obvious that the world's sign languages are still virtually virgin territory for sociolinguistic research. This study has demonstrated the usefulness of recent developments in variation theory for describing and explaining the complex variation that exists along the U. S. deaf diglossic continuum and has pointed out the urgent need to expand research in sign language variation for the deaf communities of the U. S. and the world.

APPENDIX

TABLE 45
EXCEPTIONS TO THE NEGATIVE INCORPORATION IMPLICATION

Number of People	"have"	"like"	"want"	"know"	"good"
7	+	(−)	+	+	+
1	+	(−)	+	(−)	+
1	+	(−)	(−)	+	+
1	+	+	+	+	(−)
1	−	+	+	(−)	+
1	−	+	(−)	+	+
4	−	−	+	(−)	+
1	−	−	+	+	(−)
1	−	(+)	−	−	+
1	(+)	−	−	−	+

TABLE 46
EXCEPTIONS TO THE NOT NEGATION IMPLICATION

Number of People	"good"	"know"	"want"	"like"	"have"
5	+	(−)	+	+	+
3	+	+	(−)	+	+
3	+	+	+	+	(−)
9	−	+	(−)	+	+
1	−	+	+	(−)	+
1	−	+	+	+	(−)
4	(+)	−	−	+	+
1	(+)	−	−	−	+
1	(+)	−	−	−	−
1	(+)	−	−	−	+
1	−	−	−	(+)	−

TABLE 47
EXCEPTIONS TO THE OUTWARD-INWARD AGENT-BENEFICIARY IMPLICATION

Number of People	"fingerspell"	"hate"	"hit"	"force"	"say no"	"ask"	"tell"	"give"	"show"
1	+	+	(⌒)	+	⌒	+	+	+	+
1	+	+	+	+	+	⌒	+	+	+
1	+	+	+	⌒⌒	⌒	+	⌒	+	+
4	−	+	+	+	+	+	+	+	+
4	−	+	+	+	⌒	⌒	+	+	+
2	−	+	+	⌒⌒	+	+	+	+	+
1	−	+	+	+	+	⌒	+	+	+
1	−	+	⌒	+	+	+	+	+	+
3	−	+	+	+	+	+	⌒	+	+
2	−	+	+	⌒	⌒	+	+	+	+
1	−	+	+	+	+	+	⌒⌒	⌒⌒	+
1	−	+	+	⌒	⌒	⌒	+	⌒⌒	+
1	−	+	+	+	+	+	+	+	⌒
1	−	+	+	⌒	+	+	+	+	+
1	−	+	+	+	⌒⌒	⌒	+	+	+
3	−	−	+	+	+	+	+	+	+
2	−	−	+	⌒	+	⌒	⌒⌒	+	+
1	−	−	+	+	+	+	+	+	+
1	−	−	−	+	+	⌒	⌒⌒	+	+

TABLE 47 (continued)

Number of People	"fingerspell"	"hate"	"hit"	"force"	"say no"	"ask"	"tell"	"give"	"show"
1	−	(+)	−	+	+	(−)	+	+	+
1	−	−	−	+	+	(−)	+	+	+
1	−	−	−	+	+	+	(−)	+	+
2	−	−	−	−	+	+	+	+	(−)
1	−	−	(+)	−	+	+	+	+	(−)
1	−	−	(+)	−	+	+	+	(−)	+
1	−	−	(+)	−	+	+	+	+	+
2	−	(+)	−	−	+	+	+	(−)	+
1	−	(+)	−	−	+	+	+	+	+
1	−	−	(+)	(+)	−	+	+	+	+
1	−	(+)	−	−	−	+	(−)	+	+
2	−	−	(+)	−	−	+	+	+	(−)
1	−	−	−	−	−	+	+	(−)	+
2	−	(+)	(+)	−	−	+	+	(−)	+
1	−	−	−	−	−	+	+	+	+
1	−	−	−	−	−	−	+	+	+
2	−	−	−	(+)	(+)	−	+	+	(−)
1	−	(+)	−	−	−	−	+	(−)	+
1	−	−	−	+	+	(−)	+	+	+
4	−	−	−	−	−	−	+	(−)	+

TABLE 47 (continued)

Number of People	"fingerspell"	"hate"	"hit"	"force"	"say no"	"ask"	"tell"	"give"	"show"
1	−	−	−	−	−	−	+	+	⊖
1	−	⊕	−	−	−	−	+	+	+
2	−	−	⊕	−	−	−	+	⊖	+
1	−	−	−	−	−	−	+	+	⊖
1	−	⊕	⊕	−	−	−	⊕	−	+
1	−	−	−	⊕	⊕	−	−	+	+
1	−	−	−	−	⊕	−	−	+	+
1	−	⊕	−	−	−	−	−	+	+
1	−	−	⊕	⊕ ⊕	−	−	−	+	+
1	−	−	−	−	−	⊕	−	+	+
1	−	−	⊕	−	−	−	−	+	+
2	−	−	−	⊕	−	−	−	+	+
1	−	−	⊕	−	−	⊕	−	+	+
1	−	−	⊕	−	−	+	+	+	+
5	−	−	−	−	−	⊕	−	+	+
2	−	−	−	−	−	−	−	⊕	⊖
2	−	−	−	⊕	−	−	−	⊖	⊖
1	⊕	−	−	−	−	−	−	+	−
1	−	−	⊕ ⊕	−	−	⊕	⊕	+	−
1	−	−	−	−	−	−	−	−	−
1	−	−	−	−	−	−	−	−	−
1	⊕	−	−	−	−	−	−	+	−

TABLE 48
EXCEPTIONS TO THE OUTWARD-ONLY AGENT–BENEFICIARY IMPLICATION

Number of People	"ask"	"give"	"say no"	"tell"	"force"	"hit"	"show"	"hate"	"fingerspell"
4	+	+							+
8	+	⊖	⊖	+	+	+	+	+	+
2	+	+	+	⊖	⊖	+	+	+	+
1	+	+	⊖	+		⊖	+	+	+
1	(+)	⊖	(+)	⊖	+	+	+	+	⊖
1	+	—	+	—	+	+	+	+	+
1	+	⊖	+	⊖	+	+	⊖⊖	⊖	+
1	—	⊖	+	+	+	+	+	+	+
2	—	+	+	⊖	+	⊖⊖	+	⊖	+
2	—	+	+	+	+	+	⊖⊖	+	+
2	—	+	+	+	+	⊖⊖	+	+	+
1	—	+	+	+	+	+	+	+	+
1	—	+	⊖	⊖	+	+	⊖	+	+
1	—	—	+	+	+	+	+	+	+
4	—	—	+	+	+	+	+	+	+
4	—	—	+	+	+	+	+	⊖	+
1	—	—	+	+	+	+	+	+	⊖
1	—	—	+	+	+	+	+	+	

TABLE 48 (continued)

Number of People	"ask"	"give"	"say no"	"tell"	"force"	"hit"	"show"	"hate"	"fingerspell"
1	−	−	+	(−)	+	+	+	+	(−)
1	−	−	+	+	+	+	+	(−)	(−)
1	−	−	+	+	(−)	+	+	+	(−)
1	(±)	−	+	+	(−)	+	(−)	+	+
9	−	−	−	+	+	+	+	+	+
2	−	(±)	−	+	+	(−)	+	+	+
2	(±)	−	−	+	+	+	(−)	+	+
1	−	(±)	−	+	+	+	(−)	+	+
1	−	−	−	+	+	+	(−)	(−)	+
1	−	−	−	+	+	(−)	+	(−)	+
1	(±)	−	−	+	+	+	+	+	+
1	−	−	−	−	(±)	−	+	+	+
1	−	(±)	(±)	−	+	+	+	−	+
1	−	(±)	−	−	(±)	−	(±)	+	+
1	−	(±)	−	(±)	(±)	−	+	+	+
1	−	(±)	−	−	−	+	+	+	+
1	−	−	(±)	−	−	+	+	+	+
1	−	−	−	−	−	+	+	+	+
1	−	−	−	−	−	+	+	+	(−)
1	−	−	−	−	−	−	+	(−)	+

TABLE 48 (continued)

Number	"ask"	"give"	"say no"	"tell"	"force"	"hit"	"show"	"hate"	"fingerspell" (−)
1	(+)	−	−	(+)	−	−	+	+	+
1	−	−	(+)	−	−	−	+	+	+
1	−	−	(+)	−	(+)	−	+	+	+
2	−	−	−	−	−	(+)	−	+	+
1	−	(+)	−	−	(+)	−	−	+	+
1	−	(+)	−	−	(+)	−	−	+	+
1	−	−	−	−	−	−	−	−	+
2	(+)	−	−	(+)	(+)	−	(+)	−	+
1	−	(+)	−	−	(+)	−	−	−	+
1	−	(+)	−	(+)	−	(+)	−	−	+
3	−	−	−	−	(+)	(+)	−	−	+
1	−	−	−	−	(+)	(+)	−	−	+
1	(+)	−	−	(+)	−	(+)	−	−	+
1	−	(+)	(+)	(+)	−	−	−	−	+
1	−	−	−	−	(+)	−	−	−	−

TABLE 49
EXCEPTIONS TO THE VERB REDUPLICATION IMPLICATION

Number	"meet"	"memorize"	"see"	"want"	"study"	"read"	"know"	"run"	"drive"
1	+	+	+	R	+	+	+	+	R
1	+	+	+	+	R	+	R	+	+
1	+	R	+	+	R	+	+	+	R
1	+	+	+	+	R	+	+	+	+
1	+	R	+	+	+	+	+	+	R
1	+	+	+	+	+	+	+	+	R
1	+	+	+	+	R	+	+	R	R
1	+	+	+	+	+	+	+	R	+
2	+	+	+	R	+	+	+	+	+
1	+	R	+	+	+	+	+	R	+
2	+	+	+	+	+	+	+	+	+
1	+	+	R	+	+	R	R	+	+
1	+	+	R	+	R	+	R	+	+
1	+	+	+	+	+	+	+	+	+
3	−	+	R	+	+	R	+	+	+
1	−	+	+	R	+	+	+	+	+
3	−	+	+	+	R	+	+	+	+
2	−	+	+	+	+	+	+	R	+
1	−	+	+	R	+	+	R	R	+
1	−	+	+	+	+	+	R	R	+

TABLE 49 (continued)

Number	"meet"	"memorize"	"see"	"want"	"study"	"read"	"know"	"run"	"drive"
1	−	+	+	+	+	+	+	+	⊖
1	−	+	⊖	+	+	+	+	⊖	+
2	−	−	+	+	⊖	⊖	+	+	+
1	−	−	+	+	+	+	⊖	+	+
1	−	−	+	+	+	+	+	+	⊖
1	−	−	+	+	+	⊖	+	+	+
1	⊕	⊕	−	+	⊖	+	+	+	+
1	−	−	−	+	+	+	+	+	+
2	−	−	−	+	+	+	+	+	+
2	−	−	−	+	−	+	+	⊖	+
1	⊕	⊕	−	+	+	+	+	⊖	+
1	−	⊕	−	⊕	+	+	⊖	+	+
1	−	⊕⊕	−	+	+	+	+	+	+
1	−	−	−	−	+	+	⊖	+	+
1	−	−	−	−	+	+	⊖	+	+
1	−	⊕	⊕	−	+	+	+	+	+
4	−	−	−	−	+	+	⊖⊖	+	⊖
1	−	⊕	−	−	+	+	+	+	+
2	−	−	⊕	−	+	+	+	+	⊖
1	−	−	−	−	+	+	+	+	+
1	−	−	−	−	+	+	+	+	+
1	−	−	−	−	+	⊖	+	+	+

TABLE 49 (continued)

Number	"meet"	"memorize"	"see"	"want"	"study"	"read"	"know"	"run"	"drive"
1	(+)	−	(+)	−	+	+	+	+	+
1	−	(+)	−	−	+	+	+	+	(−)
1	(+)	−	−	−	+	+	(−)	+	+
1	−	−	(+)	−	−	+	+	(−)	+
1	−	−	−	−	+	(−)	+	(−)	+
2	−	−	−	−	+	(−)	+	+	+
1	−	−	−	−	(−)	−	−	+	+
3	−	−	−	−	−	−	−	+	−
1	(+)	(+)	(+)	(+)	−	−	−	−	−
1	−	−	−	−	−	(+)	−	−	−
1	−	−	−	−	(+)	−	−	−	(+)
1	−	−	−	−	(+)	(+)	−	(+)	−
1	−	−	+	+	+	(+)	+	(+)	−
1	−	−	−	(+)	−	−	−	(+)	−
1	−	−	−	(+)	−	(+)	−	−	−
1	−	(+)	−	−	(+)	−	(+)	−	−

BIBLIOGRAPHY

Bailey, Charles-James N.
   1970 Lectal groupings in matrices generated with waves along the temporal parameter, *Working Papers in Linguistics* 2, 214.

Bailey, Charles-James N.
   1971 MS Variation and language theory.

Bailey, Charles-James N.
   1973 Personal Communication.

Battison, Robbin, Lyn Friedman, and Robert Zambrane
   1972 MS Unpublished research notes, Linguistics Research Lab.,Gallaudet College.

Battison, Robbin, and James C. Woodward, Jr.
   1972 MS Unpublished research notes, Linguistics Research Lab, Gallaudet College.

Bellugi, Ursula
   1972 Studies in Sign Language, in *Psycholinguistics and Total Communication: the state of the art*, edited by T. J. O'Rourke (Washington: The American Annals of the Deaf) 68-84.

Bergman, Eugene
   1972 Some autonomous and unique features of American Sign Language, *American Annals of the Deaf* 117:1, 20-24.

Bickerton, Derek
   1971 Inherent variability and variable rules, *Foundations of Language* 46:3, 457-492.

Bickerton, Derek
   1972 The structure of polylectal grammars,Georgetown University MSLL #25 (forthcoming).

Bloomfield, Leonard
   1933 *Language* (NY: Holt, Rinehart, and Winston).

Chomsky, Noam
   1957 *Syntactic structures* (The Hague: Mouton).

Chomsky, Noam
   1964 Comments for project literary meeting, *Project Literacy Reports* No. 2, Ithaca: Cornell University Press.

Chomsky, Noam
   1965 *Aspects of the theory of syntax* (Cambridge, Mass.: The MIT Press).

Chomsky, Noam, and Morris Halle
   1968   *The sound pattern of English*, New York: Harper and Row.

Croneberg, Carl
   1965   Sign language dialects, in *A Dictionary of American Sign Language*, Washington, DC: Gallaudet College Press 313-319.[now published by Linstok Press]

DeCamp, David
   1968 (1971) Toward a generative analysis of a post-creole speech continuum, in *Pidginization and Creolization of Languages*, edited by Dell Hymes (Cambridge: Cambridge University Press) 349-370.

DeCamp, David
   1972   What do implicational scales imply?, to appear in *New ways of analyzing variation in English*, edited by C-J N. Bailey and Roger W. Shuy (Washington, D.C.: Georgetown University Press).

DeSaussure, Ferdinand
   1959   *A course in general linguistics*, (New York: The Philosophical Library).

Donnels, Linda
   1973   New Orleans sign videotape, Linguistics Research Lab.,Gallaudet College.

Fant, Louie
   1972   *Ameslan*, (Silver Spring, Maryland: National Association of the Deaf).

Fasold, Ralph
   1970   Two models of socially significant linguistic variation, *Language* 46:3, 551-563.

Fasold, Ralph
   1972a The concept of 'earlier-later'; more or less correct, to appear in *New Ways of analyzing variation in English*, edited by C-J N. Bailey and Roger W. Shuy (Washington, D.C.: Georgetown University Press).

Fasold, Ralph
   1972b Tense marking in Black English (Washington, DC: Center for Applied Linguistics).

Ferguson, Charles
   1959   Diglossia, *Word* 15, 325-340.

Ferguson, Charles
   1972   Personal Communication.

Fishman, Joshua
   1968   *Readings in the sociology of language*, (The Hague: Mouton).

Gilleron, Jules, and Edmond Edmont
   1902-12 Atlas linguistique de la France, (Paris).

Guttman, Louis
   1944   A basis for scaling qualitative data, American Sociological Review 9, 139-150.

Hymes, Dell
   1964   Towards ethnographies of communication, in The ethnography of communication, edited by John Gumperz and Dell Hymes, American Anthropologist 66:6, 1-34.

Hymes, Dell
   1968   The ethnography of speaking, in Readings in the sociology of language, edited by Joshua Fishman, (The Hague: Mouton).

Houston, Susan
   1970   Competence and performance in child Black English, Language Sciences 12, 9-14.

Klima, Edward
   1964   Relatedness between grammatical systems, *Language* 40, 1-20.

Kurath, Hans
   1939   Handbook of the linguistic geography of New England, (providence, R.I.: Brown University Press).

Labov, William
   1963   The social motivation of a sound change, Word 19, 273-309.

Labov, William
   1969   Contraction, deletion, and inherent variability of the English copula, Language 45, 715-762.

Labov, William
   1970a   The logic of non-standard English, Georgetown University MSLL #22, 1-39.

Labov, William
   1970b   The study of language in its social context, Studium Generale 23, 30-87.

Louisanna R.I.D.
   1973   August newsletter.

Lakoff, George
   1968   Pronouns and reference (Indiana University Linguistics Club reprint).

McDavid, Raven
   1948   Postvocalic r in South Carolina: a social analysis, American Speech 23, 194-203.

Markowicz, Harry
   1972   Some sociolinguistic considerations of American Sign Language, Sign Language Studies 1, 15-41.

Meadow, Kathryn
   1972 Sociolinguistics, sign language, and the deaf sub-culture, in *Psycholinguistics and total communication: the state of the art*, edited by T. J. O'Rourke (Washington: *The American Annals of the Deaf*) 19-33.

Moores, Donald
   1972 Communication: some unanswered questions and some unquestioned answers, in *Psycholinguistics and total communication: the state of the art*, edited by T. J. O'Rourke 1-10.

O'Rourke, Terrence J.
   1970 Quoted in Stokoe, CAL conference on sign languages, LR 12:2, 5-8.

Pickford, Glenna Ruth
   1956 American linguistic geography: a sociological appraisal, Word 12, 211-233.

Ranier, J.D., K.Z. Altshuler, and F.J. Kallmann (Eds.)
   1963 Family and mental health problems in a deaf population, (New York: N.Y. State Psychiatric Institute, Columbia).

Stokoe, William C. Jr.
   1960 Sign language structure: an outline of the visual communication systems of the American deaf, Studies in Linguistics: *Occasional Paper 8*.

Stokoe, William C. Jr., C. Croneberg, and D. Casterline
   1965 A dictionary of American Sign Language, (Washington, D.C.: Gallaudet College Press).

Stokoe, William C. Jr.
   1970 Sign language diglossia, Studies in Linguistics 21, 27-41.

Stokoe, William C. Jr.
   1972a Semiotics and human sign languages, (The Hague: Mouton) Approaches to Semiotics, ed. Sebeok 21).

Stokoe, William C. Jr.
   1972b Personal communication.

Stoltz, Walter, and Garland Bills
   1968 MS An investigation of the standard-nonstandard dimension of Central Texas English

Troike, Rudolph
   1969 Overall pattern and generative phonology, in Readings in American dialectology, edited by Harold B. Allen, (New York: Appleton-Century-Croft).

Trudgill, Peter
   1972 Sex, covert prestige and linguistic change in the urban British English of Norwich, Language in Society 1:2, 179-195.

Wolfram, Walter
    1969 A sociolinguistic description of Detroit Negro speech, (Washington, D. C.: Center for Applied Linguistics).

Wolfram, Walter
    1972 On what basis variable rules? to appear in New ways of analyzing variation in English, edited by C-J N. Bailey and Roger W. Shuy, (Washington, D. C.: Georgetown University press).

Woodward, James C. Jr.
    1972 Implications for sociolinguistic research among the deaf, Sign Language Studies 1, 1-7.

Woodward, James C. Jr., and Carol Erting
    1973 Atlanta sign videotapes, Linguistics Research Laboratory, Gallaudet College.